Worlds Into Words

Worlds Into Words
Understanding Modern Poems

Diane Wood Middlebrook

W·W·NORTON & COMPANY·INC·
New York·London

Graphics on the cover and
throughout the book are by Roberta Adkins,
The Design Quarter, San Diego, California.

CREDITS

Chapter One

A. R. Ammons. "Triphammer Bridge" is reprinted from *Collected Poems 1951–1971* by A. R. Ammons. Copyright © 1972 by W.W. Norton & Company, Inc. Reprinted by permission of W.W. Norton & Company, Inc.

e.e. cummings. "l(a" is reprinted from *Complete Poems 1913–1962* by e.e. cummings. Copyright © 1958 by e.e. cummings. Reprinted by permission of Harcourt Brace Jovanovich, Inc.

Denise Levertov. An excerpt from "The Secret" is reprinted from *O Taste and See* by Denise Levertov. Copyright © 1964 by Denise Levertov Goodman. Reprinted by permission of New Directions Publishing Corporation.

Marianne Moore. An excerpt from "Poetry" is reprinted from *Collected Poems of Marianne Moore* by Marianne Moore. Copyright 1935 by Marianne Moore and renewed 1963 by Marianne Moore and T.S. Eliot. Reprinted by permission of Macmillan Publishing Company, Inc.

Ezra Pound. "Fan-Piece, for Her Imperial Lord" is reprinted from *Personae* by Ezra Pound. Copyright 1926 by Ezra Pound. Reprinted by permission of New Directions Publishing Corporation.

William Carlos Williams. "The Red Wheelbarrow," "Queen Anne's Lace," and an excerpt from "January Morning" are reprinted from *Collected Earlier Poems* by William Carlos Williams. Copyright 1938 by New Directions Publishing Corporation. Reprinted by permission of New Directions Publishing Corporation.

Chapter Two

Marcel Proust. Passages from *Remembrance of Things Past*, Volume I, by Marcel Proust, translated by C.K. Moncrieff, are reprinted by permission of Random House, Inc. Copyright 1928 and renewed 1956 by The Modern Library, Inc.

Dylan Thomas. "Fern Hill" and "Poem in October" are reprinted from *The Poems of Dylan Thomas* by Dylan Thomas. Copyright 1946 by New Directions Publishing Corporation. Reprinted by permission of New Directions Publishing Corporation.

Chapter Three

William Butler Yeats. "Sailing to Byzantium" is reprinted from *Collected Poems* by William Butler Yeats. Copyright 1928 by Macmillan Publishing Company, Inc., and renewed 1956 by Georgie Yeats. Reprinted by permission of Macmillan Publishing Company, Inc. An excerpt from "Crazy Jane Talks with the Bishop" is reprinted from *The Collected Poems of William Butler Yeats* by William Butler Yeats. Copyright 1933 by Macmillan Publishing Company, Inc. and renewed 1961 by Bertha Georgie Yeats. Reprinted by permission of Macmillan Publishing Company, Inc.

Louise Bogan. "The Alchemist" and excerpts from "Cassandra," "The Crows," "Chanson Un Peu Naïve," and "Girl's Song" are reprinted from *The Blue Estuaries* by Louise Bogan. Copyright © 1951, 1952, 1954, 1957, 1958, 1962, 1963, 1964, 1965, 1966, 1967, 1968 by Louise Bogan. Reprinted by permission of Farrar, Straus & Giroux, Inc.

For C.D.

Vix ita limitibus dissaepserunt omnia certis,
cum, quae pressa diu fuerant caligine caeca,
sidera coeperunt toto effervescere caelo.
                    from Ovid, *Metamorphoses,* I

Acknowledgments

PERSONAL THANKS are due several people who contributed substantially to the completion of this book. Jacqueline Barnett's concern with a variety of projects in the field of continuing education helped me find the appropriate voice for these essays, and her collaboration and friendship over several years gave crucial assistance when I needed it. Albert Gelpi, Barbara Gelpi, Patrick Lamb, Herbert Lindenberger, Loy Martin, Anne Mellor, and Ron Rebholz read drafts of chapters; their criticisms promoted clarity and accuracy. Irving Yalom generously permitted me to quote from a manuscript draft of his forthcoming *Existential Psychotherapy*. Long discussions with Pamela Djerassi Bush helped me probe and formulate important questions about women in art. Ingeborg Kuhn, Vern McGee, Guynn Perry, and Mary Tennes provided indispensable secretarial help, often at short notice; and Cynthia Fry Gunn's editorial advice at every stage was immensely valuable.

Table of Contents

Preface

The study of poetry is the study of life.
Wallace Stevens, from *Opus Posthumous*

THIS IS A BOOK about modern poems, written since World War I, on themes that span the human life-cycle and reflect changes in the consciousness of men and women in the twentieth century. The worlds explored in these poems are inner worlds, worlds that the poet shapes into written words. To feel at home in these worlds, it is helpful to understand how poetry is made.

Many readers approach poetry with uneasiness, unsure how to bring to the poem the special kinds of attention it seems to ask of them. Thus I have devoted the first and last chapters to a discussion of poetry as a craft. The first chapter deals with design elements in the poetic line and ways to approach the poem so that its many aspects of meaning may reveal themselves. The last chapter deals with the making of the poem, discussing a few poems of my own at various stages of completion in order to provide a window into the creative process and to clarify a poet's reasons for choosing one word or phrase over another, until the poem achieves what the poet accepts as a final statement.

Since most of the poems discussed in this book are written in free verse—that is, verse without meter—special attention is paid to principles governing the composition of various types of free verse lines. The authors are poets of great distinction, whose work has appealed to widely varied audiences: Dylan Thomas, William Butler Yeats, Louise

Bogan, Sylvia Plath, Anne Sexton, Adrienne Rich, and Theodore Roethke. But this is not primarily a book about them, nor about modern poetry in general.

The main emphasis of this book is on the study of poetry as the study of life. Words on a printed page are dead, in effect, until wakened in the vital attention of a reader; writer and reader together make the poem. Jean-Paul Sartre has described the relation between poem and reader as a collaboration. The purpose of this book is to assist in such collaborations. It offers itself as a mediator: a resource of information, observations, and interpretations meant to help each reader waken poems from the silence of print.

Diane Wood Middlebrook

Stanford, California
August 25, 1978

CHAPTER ONE

The Fear of Modern Poetry

I, too, dislike it: there are things that are important beyond all this
    fiddle.
Reading it, however, with a perfect contempt for it, one discovers in
it after all, a place for the genuine.

Marianne Moore, from "Poetry"

MARIANNE MOORE'S LINES of hesitant praise express an ambivalence toward poetry shared by many people, including those who are fascinated by it. Poetry offers us occasions to think about our feelings; it tells good stories; it rekindles delight in language. Often, it sounds beautiful. Yet the prospect of reading a poem—especially a modern poem—can alarm and distress people who are not at all afraid of prose. The very appearance of a poem on a page—print carefully arranged in lines— seems to signal the prospective reader, watch out! And the modern poet frequently compounds the threat by distributing words and lines over the page in a seemingly eccentric, even whimsical, manner.

What, then, can bring about the change of heart Marianne Moore describes, the change from impatience to fulfillment? Usually, a change in the kind of attention the reader is paying to the words. A poem rarely contains a "message" or draws a "moral" that can be stated with the

same meaning in other words. Because it is an art, poetry is not simply concerned with giving information. Yet the materials of its art are language, the common medium of information-giving. This paradox is the source of much misunderstanding about what a poet is trying to do in a poem. As W.H. Auden observes in *The Dyer's Hand,* artists who work in other media have easier public relations: "How happy the lot of the mathematician! He is judged solely by his peers, and the standard is so high that no colleague or rival can ever win a reputation he does not deserve. No cashier writes a letter to the press complaining about the incomprehensibility of Modern Mathematics and comparing it unfavorably with the good old days when mathematicians were content to paper irregularly shaped rooms."

Like any art, poetry is enjoyed most by people who know something about it. The art of poetry is a complicated form of human play, and the reader has to become one of the players in order to enjoy the art fully. Working within the confinement of self-imposed rules, the poet/reader creates an intermediate reality, one different from either fantasy, which is silently mental, hence unsharable, or the real world, where statements can have consequences and nothing is ever repeated exactly. When we are at work, words are mainly instruments, signals used to provoke or facilitate action. When we are at play as poets and readers, our relationship to words stops being automatic. We become fascinated with words for their own sake, as well as for what they can be used to say. We grow attentive to the possibilities of language and, more important, become artisans with it, exploring at leisure the byways of ambiguity and the sensuous characteristics of words.

The special relationship of the poet/reader in us to language itself is the subject of a fine contemporary poem by A.R. Ammons called "Triphammer Bridge"—a little bridge over a gorge in Ithaca, New York, viewed in the deep winter:

Triphammer Bridge

I wonder what to mean by *sanctuary,* if a real or
apprehended place, as of a bell rung in a gold
surround, or as of silver roads along the beaches

of clouds seas don't break or black mountains
overspill; jail: ice here's shapelier than anything,
on the eaves massive, jawed along gorge ledges, solid

in the plastic blue boat fall left water in: if I
think the bitterest thing I can think of that seems like
reality, slickened back, hard, shocked by rip-high wind:

sanctuary, sanctuary, I say it over and over and the
word's sound is the one place to dwell: that's it, just
the sound, and the imagination of the sound—a place.

As I read this poem over slowly several times, aloud, it becomes for me
very beautiful, a thing that seems perfectly made, that I understand,
that I believe. I wish, in fact, I had written it.

Yet I can easily imagine a reader for whom this poem would be a
perfect illustration of everything to dislike about modern poetry. Take
the form: broken syntax that leaves lines dangling, unfinished; eccentric, even incomprehensible, punctuation. Or the content (the title is, of
course, no help): once again, a poet intellectualizing about words,
taking refuge in language itself from the world of harsh reality.

The dislike such a reader feels, however, is probably based on a
number of very good questions about what Ammons is up to, why he
writes as he does. What artistic principles allow a poet to chop up
phrases in this manner? What makes such poetry any different from
prose? Does the poet really mean to be comprehensible to the average
literate person, or does he simply write for a coterie? And how does the
reader know when he or she has understood a poem like this?

These questions all arise because the poet has departed from the
norm of plain talk. The language in poetry is often at least slightly
aberrational, hence its power to arouse anxiety. Reading poetry, then,
requires an understanding of the poet's methods and intentions. And
reading poetry expertly can lead the mind to that experience peculiar to
art which Ammons likens to "sanctuary" and Wallace Stevens, in *The
Necessary Angel,* to "liberation": "Anyone who has read a long poem
day after day . . . knows how the poem comes to possess the reader and
how it naturalizes him in its own imagination and liberates him there."

In quest of that valuable experience, I shall discuss in the next few pages how poetry differs from other kinds of writing.

What Makes Poetry Different from Prose?

> All this—
>   was for you, old woman.
> I wanted to write a poem
> that you would understand.
> For what good is it to me
> if you can't understand it?
>   But you got to try hard—
>
> William Carlos Williams, from "January Morning"

Definitions of poetry can be found in many contexts; most likely, each poet has his or her own. I prefer this very simple working definition: poetry is *deliberate speech, presented in lines*.

All written language is deliberate. The poet, however—unlike other writers—deliberates not only about which words to use, but also about how many of them belong in a *line*. The line is the definitive unit of composition in poetry—the one characteristic that truly differentiates poetry from prose. The way words fall on a page of prose usually depends on the typesetter. But each line-ending in a poem represents the poet's active choice. The line-ending is the place where the poem offers itself as a work of art different from every other kind of art.

To call poetry deliberate speech is to stress, further, that poetry always contains a voice. Even a computer printout has a human author, however well-concealed in its instrumental diction. But poetry always acknowledges and makes the most of its sensuous origins. Someone, however impalpable, is always speaking in a poem, and individual subjectivity is an aspect of the poem's meaning.

What Makes a Line?

Study of the technical aspects of poetry, called prosody, is mainly a concern of scholars. However, knowing about the kind of decision-making that goes into the creation of a line of poetry can increase a reader's appreciation of the care a poet takes in adapting sense to sound. The following remarks are offered as guides to close reading, to help the reader identify as distinct the units that compose the poem, to make them units of attention.

Rhythm and Meter. Rhythm is a product of variation in sounds. In speech, rhythm is produced by differences in the duration of sounds in words, differences in stresses on syllables within words, differences in the sounds vowels and consonants make, and differences in pauses.

Normal talk is rhythmic in a haphazard way; poetry is rhythmic in an organized way. Rhythm that is highly organized into recurring patterns is called meter. All poetry is rhythmic, but only some is metrical. Because meter is a pattern rather than an effect, it is possible to distinguish among metrical types.

Metered rhythm is measured in poetic feet. A poetic foot contains either two or three syllables, only one of which is stressed (´). Metrical types are identified by:

- the *kind* of poetic foot that dominates a line of metered poetry:
  iambic: two syllables, unstressed-stressed (˘ ´)
  trochaic: two syllables, stressed-unstressed (´ ˘)
  anapestic: three syllables, unstressed-unstressed-stressed (˘ ˘ ´)
  dactylic: three syllables, stressed-unstressed-unstressed (´ ˘ ˘)
  (occasionally, a fifth kind of poetic foot appears—*spondaic:* two syllables, both stressed (´ ´); a spondee is used chiefly as a variation, substituting for an iamb or a trochee)

- the *number* of poetic feet in a line of metered poetry:

monometer (one foot)	*tetrameter* (four feet)
dimeter (two feet)	*pentameter* (five feet)
trimeter (three feet)	*hexameter* (six feet)

"Sailing to Byzantium" by William Butler Yeats (see Chapter Three) is, for example, a poem in meter; it has iambic pentameter lines with frequent substitutions of trochees:

> Thát is / no cóun / try fór / óld men. / The yóung
> In ońe / anó / ther's árms, / birds in / the trées
> —Those dy / ing gé / nerá / tions—át / their sóng.

"The Alchemist" by Louise Bogan (Chapter Three) is written in iambic tetrameter, with occasional substitutions of trochees and spondees and one "headless" line, where a pause takes the place of an unstressed syllable:

> I búrned / my life, / that Í / might find
> A pás / sion whól / ly óf / the mind,
> Thoúght / divórced / from eýe / and bóne.
> Écsta / sy cóme / to bréath / alońe.
> I bróke / my life / to séek / relief
> From the / flawed líght / of lóve / and gríef.

Most of the poems discussed in this book, however, are nonmetrical; they are examples of poems written in free verse.

Rhythm and Free Verse. Free verse is a relatively recent invention. Although William Blake and Walt Whitman in some of their poetry used a free verse line modeled on the Psalms, free verse did not gain wide acceptance until around the time of World War I, when poetry underwent a radical transformation and became distinctively modern in its appearance. Free verse, as its users testify, is not so much "free" as nonmetrical in its structure. The syllables are arranged as carefully as they are in metered verse, but the decisions about where to end the line are based on different principles. According to literary critic Charles Rosen, in the techniques of composition leading to free verse, "minute attentiveness to words replaces the coercive rhythm of older poetic styles"; the poet "renounces communication for presentation."

There are basically three kinds of free verse: syllabic free verse, accentual free verse, and free verse composed in units of syntax.

The most common kind of free verse is that in which the line-ending corresponds to the *unit of syntax.* An example occurs in William Carlos Williams's "January Morning," quoted earlier:

> All this—
>   was for you, old woman.
> I wanted to write a poem
> that you would understand.

In each line Williams completes a grammatical phrase, not breaking up the syntax as Ammons does in "Triphammer Bridge" ("if a real or / apprehended place, as of a bell rung in a gold / surround"), where adjectives are frequently separated from the nouns they modify, and subjects are separated from their predicates ("black mountains / overspill"; "if I / think of the bitterest thing"). Ammons's poem is, in fact, representative of another type, *accentual* free verse.

In accentual free verse, each line contains a certain number of heavily stressed syllables that are not arranged with metrical regularity. "Triphammer Bridge" is composed in lines ranging from nine to eighteen syllables in length, with five to eight receiving heavy stress. Ammons avoids sounding as if he intended a repeating metrical pattern, however, by distributing the stresses unevenly, often jamming several stressed syllables together in one part of the line:

> of clóuds séas don't bréak or bláck móuntains
> óverspíll; jáil: íce heŕe's shápelier than ánythíng.

Ammons's lines in "Triphammer Bridge" are fairly long. Accentual free verse lines may also be short, sometimes very short, as in this poem by William Carlos Williams.

The Red Wheelbarrow

so múch depénds
upón

a réd whéel
bárrow

glázed with ráin
wáter

besíde the whíte
chíckens.

The stresses fall in a pattern of two heavy stresses (múch, -pénds) followed by one (-ón); two, then one; two, then one; two, then one. Units of syntax are systematically broken at the end of each longer line, producing an effect of great deliberateness. Each syllable attains exceptional prominence by having so little competition for our attention in each line. Literary critic Hugh Kenner, in *A Homemade World,* describes free verse based on this short-line model as "small change, symmetrically counted."

A third type is *syllabic* free verse. Form in syllabic verse is established by counting syllables and keeping the stresses from falling in regular metrical patterns. English versions of the Japanese haiku form are a well-known type of syllabic free verse. The haiku in English is composed of three lines containing a fixed number of syllables, usually seventeen or nineteen. This poem by Ezra Pound is an example:

Fan-Piece, for Her Imperial Lord

O fan of white silk,
        clear as frost on the grass-blade,
You also are laid aside.

Dylan Thomas's "Poem in October" (see Chapter Two) is also in syllabics; the first stanza establishes the norm that the others strictly follow.

Rhythm and Typography. A discussion of the arrangement of sound in creating rhythm would be incomplete without consideration of the role that silence plays. Poet Charles Olson speculates in his essay "Projective Verse" (in *Human Universe*) that the use of free verse became widespread at about the time the typewriter became widely available because the machine encouraged the poet to think of the line as filling precise amounts of *space*: "It is the advantage of the typewriter that, due to its rigidity and its space precisions, it can, for a poet, indicate exactly the breath, the pauses, the suspensions even of syllables, the juxtapositions even of parts of phrases, which he intends. . . . For the first time he can . . . record the listening he has done to his own speech and by that one act indicate how he would want any reader, silently or otherwise, to voice his work."

Some of the most visible differences between modern and traditional poetry have been created by ingenious use of space on the page. The major innovator in this regard was e.e. cummings, whose typographical oddities were a way of forcing attention to the most molecular aspects of communication (including the convention of capitalizing names). In cummings's line, the unit of attention may become very small indeed, even less than a syllable sometimes:

l(a

l(a

le
af
fa

ll

s)
one
l

iness

Of course, traditional meters, in the hands of artisans, make full and supple use of pauses as a means of variation within regular sound patterns. But free verse, which is by intention metrically irregular, also uses the pause to affect the rhythm. Silences are orchestrated, like syllables, in the free verse line. It is important to know, then, that poets whose lines appear visually eccentric are communicating something quite precise and readable from their point of view. Again in his essay "Projective Verse," Charles Olson describes this precision:

If a contemporary poet leaves a space as long as the phrase before it, he means that space to be held, by the breath, an equal length of time. If he suspends a word or syllable at the end of a line . . . he means that time to pass that it takes the eye—that hair of time suspended—to pick up the next line. If he wishes a pause so light it hardly separates the words, yet does not want a comma—which is an interruption of the meaning rather than the sounding of the line—follow him when he uses a symbol the typewriter has ready to hand:

> What does not change / is the will to change

Observe him, when he takes advantage of the machine's multiple margins, to juxtapose:

> Sd he:
>   to dream takes no effort
>   to think is easy
>   to act is more difficult
>   but for a man to act after he has taken thought, this!
>   is the most difficult thing of all

Each of these lines is a progressing of both the meaning and the breathing forward, and then a backing up, without a progress or any kind of movement outside the unit of time local to the idea.

Not all poets use the interior slash or the variable margin as Olson does, or would agree with Olson's idea that line length should or can be correlated with exhalations of breath. But all poets intend that the pauses they create, by means of spacing words and by the placement of line-endings, be understood as design elements in the poem.

Unfolding a Modern Poem: Completing the Poet's Creation

Two girls discover
the secret of life
in a sudden line of
poetry.

I who don't know the
secret wrote
the line.

Denise Levertov, from "The Secret"

Even though it is presented in lines, a modern poem is nonlinear in its form of communication. As Olson's remarks suggest, the beginning and the end are part of a continuous whole. Ideally, the end of the poem should send the reader back to the beginning, to see how the beginning and the ending are related to each other and how everything in between is essential to both. The poem is more like a loop than a line. Or, to borrow A.R. Ammons's lovely phrase, each syllable is like "a bell rung in a gold surround": together syllables chime and resonate with one another, revealing the kinds of "secrets" Denise Levertov's delighted readers found, hidden even from the poet. For the progress of thought in a modern poem does not lead to the formulation of correct answers, as in mathematics; nor does it lead to judgments, as in law; or to causal expositions of events, such as those structured by the journalist's questions *who-what-when-where-how.*

These differences hold even when the poem, like "Triphammer Bridge," is partially concerned with making judgments ("I say it over and over and the / word's sound is the one place to dwell: that's it, just / the sound"), or with describing things and events ("ice here's shapelier than anything, / on the eaves massive, jawed along gorge ledges, solid / in the plastic blue boat fall left water in"). In the poem, beginning and end are design elements, something like boundaries, or the edges of a frame. They define the space of the poem, the zone of attention, in which words and phrases occur in various kinds of relation to each other, including the relation of their sounds.

To emphasize the spatial aspect of the poem, Olson describes the act of making modern poetry elsewhere in "Projective Verse" as "composition by field"—a field of force such as a magnetic field, in which the charged particles are syllables and phrases. What the poet makes in this field are not statements, but syntheses of meaning. "Triphammer Bridge" provides good examples of this process: here, ice enters the speaker's field of vision ("ice here's shapelier than anything"); it also enters the field of composition established by the problem on the speaker's mind—sanctuary, or rather, "what to mean by *sanctuary*." Seeking a meaning for sanctuary has led him to thoughts of various kinds of protected spaces and their boundaries: the "gold surround" enclosing a bell; the silver linings of clouds; jail—a more ambiguously protective enclosure. Ice, too, outlines the boundaries of things, but not in a way analogous to "sanctuary." "Massive," "jawed," "solid" ice shifts into the zone of negative forces in the poem—the things one needs sanctuary *from*. Finally the sound of the word itself—like the sound of a bell rung—becomes a refuge. The meaning sought outside the word is discovered within it when "sanctuary" moves from the plane of abstraction to something heard, grasped by the senses.

"Triphammer Bridge" is an example of <u>nonlinear thinking</u>, then, because even though the poet arrives in the poem at a definition that satisfies him, the definition itself is not the point of the poem. The point is *making* the definition, recreating the movements of thought and *aleatory* feeling by which the poet arrives at the sense, "that's it." The poem is therefore not a statement but a model: of a mind in the act of seeking, and finding, personal significance in a general idea. This being the case, reading a poem requires a particular kind of attention. As Williams says, "You got to try hard." It takes training, because, although reading is a very common activity, reading poetry demands uncommon alertness.

Granted a willingness to try hard, how does one go about grasping a poem as profoundly as do Levertov's readers in "The Secret"? The formal methodologies applied to the acts of understanding a poem are called explication, from the Latin *explicare,* to unfold. In explicating a poem we unfold it part by part, examining each aspect until we have accounted, to our satisfaction, for the whole. The term *explicate* has the same cognate as does the word *ply*: like yarn, a poem may be regarded as a composite of webbed strands that we can distinguish and untangle from each other. For example, within the same phrase, aspects of rhythm and aspects of imagery may be distinguished from each other, as in the lines from "Triphammer Bridge": "ice here's shapelier than anything, / on the eaves massive, jawed along gorge ledges." Visualizing the way massed ice edges roofs and transforms a gorge into the semblance of a jawbone requires an act of attention different from that involved in listening to the recurrent sounds *eaves, -sive; jaw, -orge, -edge.* Having performed these separate acts of unfolding, one can return to the line prepared to hear how its sound assists in the making of meanings.

As the terms explicate and ply suggest, the reader's relationship to the poem should be that of the unfolder who takes hold of the poem at various levels, segregating not line from line but aspect from aspect. In this undertaking literary criticism recognizes four lines of inquiry, each distinct from the other. The four lines of inquiry may be compared to lenses with different focal lengths, each used to inspect a different aspect of the poem. One lens fixes our attention on the poem as autonomous, as a thing in itself. The other three view the poem in relation to other things: its maker, its literary and cultural context, and the individual reader. In the next few pages I shall demonstrate how these four different lenses—called autonomous, contextual, biographical, and affective—can be used to give the reader a view of the poem with all detail in clear focus. Here, first, is a poem:

Queen Anne's Lace

Her body is not so white as
anemone petals nor so smooth—nor
so remote a thing. It is a field
of the wild carrot taking
the field by force; the grass
does not raise above it.
Here is no question of whiteness,
white as can be, with a purple mole
at the center of each flower.
Each flower is a hand's span
of her whiteness. Wherever
his hand has lain there is
a tiny purple blemish. Each part
is a blossom under his touch
to which the fibres of her being
stem one by one, each to its end,
until the whole field is a
white desire, empty, a single stem,
a cluster, flower by flower,
a pious wish to whiteness gone over—
or nothing.

First Lens: Seeing the Poem as Autonomous

I shall begin by pretending I do not know who wrote these lines and do not know the writer's sex or age. For those details belong, if they are relevant at all, to the line of inquiry relating the poem to its maker. I will also forget, for a while, the date of composition, and ignore the audience to whom the poem was addressed. Reference to the world outside the poem employs the approach I labeled "contextual." Finally, I will try not to emphasize what personally attracted me to the poem and made me wish to write about it, for these considerations belong to the "affective" aspects of the poem in its relation to me.

Two or three careful readings without reference to any outside source (except a dictionary) allow me to discern the following meanings in the poem.

The beginning of "Queen Anne's Lace" is almost hesitant, as if the poet were looking at a woman with an eye to putting her in a poem based on comparisons between women and flowers. Her body is not so white as—as—ah! anemone petals. Anemone petals rather resemble flesh. But not her flesh. Departing from convention the poet seizes on a common weed as the truer likeness to what he wants to describe; and as the likeness grows lucid, the tone grows more definite. The repeated use of "is" gives an almost clinical voice to the middle of the poem. In the last nine lines, the rhythm changes again. When the man's hand enters the image, the poet's tone grows less detached and the pace accelerates. The poet keeps to the form established in the opening lines—accentual free verse alternating between three and four stresses per line. But the references to blossoming and stemming introduce a heightened feeling of attentiveness. And the rhythmic repetitions of sound, like repeated strokes of a hand, build—for my ear—a sense of tension, of reaching a climax of total involvement, then release.

The whole poem can be seen, on second reading, as an extended comparison between a field of weeds (Queen Anne's lace, also called wild carrot) and the sexually aroused body of a woman. The construction of the lines emphasizes the growing urgency the poem describes. The poem works by identifying the woman's body with a field of flowers *viewed as a field of force:*

> Each part
> is a blossom under his touch
> to which the fibres of her being
> stem one by one, each to its end.

"Span," "blossom," "cluster," even "flower" are nouns that convey action and may be used as verbs; and throughout, the flowers themselves are treated not as objects but as processes:

> a field
> of the wild carrot taking
> the field by force . . .
> . . . .
> until the whole field is a
> white desire.

Second Lens: Viewing the Poem in Its Contexts

"Queen Anne's Lace," like most of the other poems treated in this book, can be read without the aid of footnotes. To understand it, we need to know only what is given on the page (though it is helpful to have lived in a place where Queen Anne's lace is a common weed). Yet the poem grows richer when the reader is able to view it in other perspectives: its context in the world of literature and its context in the world of its cultural contemporaries. The more one reads poetry, the easier this becomes.

The Context of Literature. To approach the poem in its context as literature means thinking about its similarities to other written works, thinking in terms of analogies. "Queen Anne's Lace" lends itself to this approach because it is, from one point of view, a conventional poem. That is, it has some of the characteristics of a type—a poem in which a woman is compared to a flower, as in Robert Burns's "My love is like a red, red rose." From this type of poem—which emerges from the tradition of courtly love poetry in which a chief activity of poets was praising women—we have come to expect an idealizing attitude on the part of the poet. But the poet in "Queen Anne's Lace" slyly rejects that aspect of the convention in the opening lines, where he refuses the possibility of a comparison with anemone petals as too remote; for "her body is not so white . . . / . . . nor so smooth." In turning the convention on its head, the poet both reminds us of the tradition and refuses to be part of it—rather as Shakespeare does in his anticonventional sonnet "My mistress' eyes are nothing like the sun":

> I have seen roses damasked, red and white,
> But no such roses see I in her cheeks;
> And in some perfumes is there more delight
> Than in the breath that from my mistress reeks.

The poet's perception of the woman's body as "a field / of the wild carrot" thus has some shock value. But by the end of the poem this particular flower stands fully disclosed as identical with a woman's passion. The poet has idealized the wild carrot in the most literal sense—by describing the clustery flower in terms equating it with the idea of aroused sexual desire.

"Queen Anne's Lace" belongs also to another poetic tradition: poetry on the subject of *metamorphosis,* or transformation. In Western art the archetype of poetry in this genre is Ovid's *Metamorphoses,* which deals ambitiously with a whole range of Greek and Roman myths in which gods and men change forms: the god Zeus becomes a bull; the man Tiresias becomes a woman; the maiden Clytie becomes a sunflower; and so forth. *Metamorphoses* has influenced writers for centuries, as a source of stories and also as an expression of a theory of art. The poet, as artist, is the agent of metamorphosis: poetry becomes the transformation of *things* into *meanings.* In Ovid's story of Clytie, for example, a mortal woman is transformed into an emblem of her unrequited love for the sun god—a sunflower, a living form with its roots in the earth and its face continually turned toward heaven. Clytie was mortal, like all maidens, but the poet—like a god—gives her a symbolic form that expresses the meaning of her brief existence. *Metamorphoses* is myth-making poetry, and so, in a less explicit way, is "Queen Anne's Lace." In the course of the poet's realizations of the idea "white desire," we watch a woman's body come into focus as the stemming energies of a field of wild flowers. The flowers themselves become, vividly, symbols of pure desire—or nothing: mere flowers, mere objects without significance. At this mythic level, the poem acquires yet another meaning. It expresses an identification of a woman's eroticism with the stemming, blossoming aspects of nature revealed in a flower's responsiveness to warmth and light. It is a myth affirming the human connection with the processes of nature.

This mythic, or timeless, aspect of the poem's meaning may not have been part of the poet's original design. For one of the paradoxes of literary creation allows that the published text may initiate processes over which the poet can have no further control. Because it is literature, the poem may present itself in ways that may not have been on the poet's mind but may come quite legitimately to the reader's mind.

The Context of the Poem's Contemporaries. Up to this point I have withheld, with some difficulty, any reference to the author of "Queen Anne's Lace" except as its maker, "the poet." At this point the author must be identified, because this poet has to a great extent created the very milieu of which this poem is a part. To speak of contemporary American poetry is to imply his way of writing.

William Carlos Williams is the author. The poem appeared in 1923, a time when British and American poetry was undergoing radical change, largely through the efforts of Ezra Pound, T.S. Eliot, and Williams himself. Pound and Williams were good friends, and Williams early in his career embraced Pound's revolutionary vision in the field of aesthetics. This vision came to be known as Imagism. In brief, Imagism was a movement away from the didactic, moralizing, and emotionally effusive kinds of poetry being written in the post-Victorian, pre-World War I period. Pressed for a rationalization of the difference between Imagism and other kinds of poetry, Pound (in *Poetry* magazine, March 1913) came up with a definition: the image, essence of the Imagist poem, was "that which presents an intellectual and emotional complex in an instant of time." Pound's collaborator F.S. Flint, in the same issue of *Poetry,* stated a set of rules. In writing a poem, Flint said, the Imagist followed certain guidelines:

1. Direct treatment of the "thing" whether subjective or objective.
2. To use absolutely no word that does not contribute to the presentation.
3. As regarding rhythm: to compose in the sequence of the musical phrase, not in sequence of a metronome.

"Queen Anne's Lace" is an excellent example of this technique: a poem in free verse in which the subject—desire—is treated directly, through its total identification with a thing—the appearance of a field, the shape of a flower. One aspect of directness in Imagism was the diminished role of the poet's personality in the poem. In Williams's poem there is no "I"; the poet presents objects, not himself: the wild carrot remains in plain sight. Brevity and the avoidance of meter also enhance the feeling of concentration on the object.

Imagism, then, lies visibly in the cultural context of "Queen Anne's Lace" and provides some of its meanings. Equally but less visibly in the background lies Williams's ideological quarrel with other kinds of poetry that evolved from Imagism but used Imagist techniques of suggestion and juxtaposition for different poetic ends. In particular, "Queen Anne's Lace" can be seen as an alternative to the kinds of poetry written by the allusive Pound and the erudite Eliot. In his *Autobiography,* looking back over forty years or so as a poet, Williams singled out the publication of Eliot's *The Waste Land* in 1922 as an important watershed in the development of modern poetry:

> It wiped out our world as if an atom bomb had been dropped upon it and our brave sallies into the unknown were turned to dust.
>
> To me especially it struck like a sardonic bullet. I felt at once that it had set me back twenty years, and I'm sure it did. Critically Eliot returned us to the classroom just at the moment when I felt that we were on the point of an escape to matters much closer to the essence of a new art form itself—rooted in the locality which should give it fruit. . . .
>
> Eliot had turned his back on the possibility of reviving my world. And being an accomplished craftsman, better skilled in some ways than I could ever hope to be, I had to watch him carry my world off with him, the fool, to the enemy.

The key phrase in Williams's emphatic statement is that art should be *rooted in locality.* Unlike Pound and Eliot, whose art reflects belief in cultural universals, Williams chose to stay out of the classrooms of religion, myth, and history; he chose instead plain-speaking in American idioms, following the example of the first distinguishably American poet, Walt Whitman. Williams also wrote poetry that, like Whitman's, tries to capture the feeling of locale and the common life. In "Queen Anne's Lace," for example, Williams chose a weed common to the American Northeast and, further, preferred putting a wild flower in his poem rather than the cultivated anemone.

This artistic philosophy was probably not the consequence of a narrow chauvinism but of Williams's recognition that his own talent lay in catching glimpses of the world in memorably concrete terms. He taught, by example, how to write a poetry of minute attentiveness; in doing so, he exerted an extraordinary influence on contemporary poetry. "No ideas but in things" was his lifelong credo. "Queen Anne's Lace" may thus be viewed as one manifestation of a whole way of making art: a radical document from a productive period of ferment in poetry by one of the leaders of the revolution.

Third Lens: The Poem in Relation to Its Author

Thus far I have been discussing Williams's contributions as an artist to the world of modern poetry, and the way his theories about art are exemplified in "Queen Anne's Lace." I called this a contextual, rather than a biographical, perspective on the poem because it involves viewing Williams in a wholly public role. But one could, hypothetically, also view "Queen Anne's Lace" from the point of view of the poet's biography, observing its characteristics not as an expression of a theory of poetry but as an expression of a man's life—looking into the man's unique experiences to find traces of the poem's sources and private meanings.

"Queen Anne's Lace," unlike most of the poems treated in the following chapters, is not a poem that yields much to this kind of scrutiny. Dylan Thomas, for example, makes his own childhood the direct subject of "Fern Hill" (see Chapter Two), and what we can learn from outside sources about that childhood and that place enrich our readings of the poem. Adrienne Rich (see Chapter Four) records throughout her poetry a strained course of self-development, so that successive books of her poems read like chapters in an unfinished autobiography. But "Queen Anne's Lace" does not even contain a single "I" to look at, and few of the facts of Williams's life are even faintly relevant to an understanding of the poem.

Still, poetry, unlike some other forms of writing, is inevitably personal. However careful the poet may be to keep himself out of the poem— and Williams is very careful about that—the poem originates in the consciousness of a living man or woman, and the language of poetry reveals this origin. Hence, I can see how a discussion of "Queen Anne's Lace" might figure in a critical biography of Williams, as exemplifying the nature of the imaginative receptivity crucial to Williams's art. The argument might go like this:

"Queen Anne's Lace" presents an image of a woman in a state of sexual arousal. But the erotic often appears in art as a concrete way of talking about something else: a religious person's mystical experience of God, or other experiences eliciting a totality of response. Sexual response is only one basis for imagery of receptivity; others might be eating (as when we speak of digesting and absorbing a page of print, or chewing things over), breathing (as when we speak of being inspired), even seeing (as when we speak of regarding, observing, or gathering impressions)—all of which imply openness rather than intrusiveness.

Hence, when poets try to describe their own experiences of the creative process, they often resort to physically charged imagery to convey a preliminary stage of creative consciousness involving *taking things in.* Denise Levertov's remarks in "Some Notes on Organic Form," from her book *The Poet in the World,* offer a good example. Levertov writes that the origin of a poem, in her experience, is a feeling of domination by a demand, and that

the beginning of the fulfillment of this demand is to contemplate, to meditate; words which connote a state in which the heat of feeling warms the intellect. To contemplate comes from "*templum,* temple, a place, a space for observation, marked out by the augur." It means, not simply to observe, to regard, but to do these things in the presence of a god. And to meditate is "to keep the mind in a state of contemplation"; its synonym is "to muse," and to muse comes from a word meaning "to stand with open mouth"—not so comical if we think of "inspiration"—to breathe in.

In the light of these observations it is possible to view "Queen Anne's Lace" as a poem about the poet's capacity for passionate attention. In this interpretation, the woman's response to touch would be analogous to the poet's rapt contemplation of the object of his poem, when, under the influence of inner imperatives, he places himself solely at the poem's disposal, to bring about its culmination in language.

Fourth Lens: The Reader's Response

The fourth lens, or line of inquiry, looks at the poem's effects on its audiences. Of course, from one point of view, a poem cannot be said to exist at all except within the consciousness of a reader. As Jean-Paul Sartre observes in *What Is Literature?* when we praise a literary work for its lifelike characters, we are really praising our own abilities to enliven them: "The grandiosity of *Armance,* the degree of realism and truth of Kafka's mythology, these are never given. The reader must invent them all in a continual exceeding of the written thing. To be sure, the author guides him, but all he does is guide him. . . . The work exists only at the exact level of [the reader's] capacities; while he reads and creates, he knows that he can always go further in his reading, can always create more profoundly, and thus the work seems to him as inexhaustible and opaque as things." The writer undertakes a revelation that the reader completes: "Since the artist must entrust to another the job of carrying out what he has begun, . . . all literary work is an appeal."

Thus even while trying to write "objectively" about William Carlos Williams's "Queen Anne's Lace," I necessarily write of its meanings to me. The point is that all interpretation of poetry begins in the poem's appeal to the reader's own existence, in the poem's power to excite the reader's desire to know more perceptively, to challenge and extend the reader's capacities. In the preceding pages I have been attempting to assist the reader to engage in that full participation in the poem's creation by sketching a rough map of poetry as territory different from other kinds of writing, and to suggest routes into the least accessible areas. A few last words might be offered about the act of reading itself.

First, it is essential to read each poem more than once. As with the enjoyment of music, the comprehension of poetry depends on familiarity. "In my end is my beginning," T.S. Eliot wrote of the structure of *Four Quartets;* the same is true of all poems. In repeated readings the poem's design begins to disclose itself. The more fully the reader possesses the poem, the more it means.

Second, each poem should be read aloud, and slowly. Though there are exceptions to the rule, poetry is written for the ear as well as for the eye. The poems included in this book should be heard to be fully appreciated, for the language of the poem is measured and rhythmical, and the rhythms are guides to subtleties of feeling and meaning. Though reading aloud is an art, it is easy to learn. The important thing is to read slowly, pausing as punctuation indicates—including a pause at the end of each line—briefly if the line-ending is unpunctuated, longer if punctuated. Even when the sense of the poem flows over into the next line, the line-ending is always an important place, and a reader should pay attention to it by pausing, however slightly. As the meaning of the poem reveals itself to the reader through repeated readings, it also reveals itself in the responsiveness of the reader's voice.

The chapters that follow present ambitious and beautiful poems exploring many universal themes. No more need be said in preparation. The poems themselves await us, at the exact level of our capacities to complete their creation.

"In the sun born over and over,
I ran my heedless ways,"

CHAPTER TWO

Summoning Childhood: Poetry of Dylan Thomas

Time held me green and dying
Though I sang in my chains like the sea.

Dylan Thomas, from "Fern Hill"

ONE OF THE MOST IMPORTANT BOOKS in modern literature issues un-
forgettably from a memory of childhood, when a man in the middle of
life, exhausted by a boredom which resembles despair, involuntarily
recalls a moment from the past:

> One day in winter, as I came home, my mother, seeing that I
> was cold, offered me some tea, a thing I did not ordinarily
> take. I declined at first, and then, for no particular reason,
> changed my mind. She sent out for one of those short, plump
> little cakes called "petites madeleines," which look as though
> they had been moulded in the fluted scallop of a pilgrim's
> shell. And soon, mechanically, weary after a dull day with the
> prospect of a depressing morrow, I raised to my lips a spoon-
> ful of the tea in which I had soaked a morsel of the cake. No
> sooner had the warm liquid, and the crumbs with it, touched
> my palate than a shudder ran through my whole body, and I

stopped, intent upon the extraordinary changes that were taking place. An exquisite pleasure had invaded my senses, but individual, detached, with no suggestion of its origin. And at once the vicissitudes of life had become indifferent to me, its disasters innocuous, its brevity illusory—this new sensation having had on me the effect which love has of filling me with a precious essence; or rather this essence was not in me, it was myself. I had ceased now to feel mediocre, accidental, mortal. Whence could it have come to me, this all-powerful joy? I was conscious that it was connected with the taste of tea and cake, but that it infinitely transcended these savours, could not, indeed, be of the same nature as theirs. Whence did it come? What did it signify? How could I seize upon and define it? . . .

And suddenly the memory returns. The taste was that of the little crumb of madeleine which on Sunday mornings at Combray . . . when I went to say good day to her in her bedroom, my aunt Léonie used to give me, dipping it first in her own cup of real or of lime-flower tea. . . . And just as the Japanese amuse themselves by filling a porcelain bowl with water and steeping in it little crumbs of paper which until then are without character or form, but, the moment they become wet, stretch themselves and bend, take on colour and distinctive shape, become flowers or houses or people, permanent and recognisable, so in that moment all the flowers in our garden and in M. Swann's park, and the water-lilies on the Vivonne and the good folk of the village and their little dwellings and the parish church and the whole of Combray and of its surroundings, taking their proper shapes and growing solid, sprang into being, town and gardens alike, from my cup of tea.

This account of an actual event appears in the opening chapter, "Overture," of Marcel Proust's eight-volume masterpiece, *Remembrance of Things Past*. The novel is autobiographical; appropriately, it opens with the earliest childhood memories that can be fitted into a coherent pattern. Yet the reference to childhood in this passage has a double purpose, which Proust makes clear. His novel begins with a scene reclaimed from the past not only in order to begin at the beginning of his own existence in time, but also because the scene recaptured reflects the earliest stage of the symbol-making capacity, which is the origin of all art and one of our mental powers attained long before intellectual mastery. The intensity of this memory affirms that the Sunday ritual of tasting his aunt's morning pastry already had for the child a richness of perceived associations, an imaginative structure. As the memory slowly clarifies within him, the bored, depressed adult undergoes a transformation: "I had ceased to feel mediocre, accidental, mortal." The mind he has resumed—the mind continuous with the child he was—is a mind to which the most common events of life stand revealed in their supreme importance. He has recaptured, in the depths of his being, an ability to apprehend what he boldly calls the soul in things, which he had discovered as a child and which has been waiting to be rediscovered through his senses of smell and taste:

> I feel that there is much to be said for the Celtic belief that the souls of those whom we have lost are held captive in some inferior being, in an animal, in a plant, in some inanimate object, and so effectively lost to us until the day (which to many never comes) when we happen to pass by the tree or to obtain possession of the object which forms their prison. Then they start and tremble, they call us by our name, and as soon as we have recognised their voice the spell is broken. We have delivered them: they have overcome death and return to share our life.
>
> And so it is with our own past. It is a labour in vain to attempt to recapture it: all the efforts of our intellect must prove futile. The past is hidden somewhere outside the realm, beyond the reach of intellect, in some material object (in the sensation which that material object will give us) which we do not suspect. . . . But when from a long-distant past nothing subsists, after the people are dead, after the things are broken and scattered, still, alone, more fragile, but with more vitality, more unsubstantial, more persistent, more faithful, the smell and taste of things remain poised a long time, like souls, ready to remind us, waiting and hoping for their moment, amid the ruins of all the rest; and bear unfaltering, in the tiny and almost impalpable drop of their essence, the vast structure of recollection.

Elaborating in prose the vast structure of his recollection became Proust's whole vocation from 1909 until his death in 1922. *Remembrance of Things Past* is thus a work contemporary with the middle work of Freud, who died in 1939. However, the meaning of the onset of memory in Proust's novel is very different from what its meaning would be in the case history of a person undergoing psychoanalysis. For Proust has retrieved, from a mouthful of tea, not a traumatic secret hidden from consciousness, but an ordinariness with infinite value: an image, like the images of art. Here, his own memory has been the artist. Yet in the course of his imaginative pursuit of that initially undecipherable joy, Proust realizes that he has stumbled upon the key to the relationship between experience and art:

> The potion is losing its magic. It is plain that the object of my quest, the truth, lies not in the cup but in myself. . . . I put down my cup and examine my own mind. It is for it to discover the truth. But how? What an abyss of uncertainty whenever the mind feels that some part of it has strayed beyond its own borders; when it, the seeker, is at once the dark region through which it must go seeking, where all its equipment will avail it nothing. Seek? More than that: create. It is face to face with something which does not so far exist, to which it alone can give reality and substance, which it alone can bring into the light of day.

The recognition that the object of his quest lies within himself forms the bridge between the silent joy of memory and the speaking voice of Proust's novel. For, Proust reasons, if total recall through involuntary memory has the power truly to redeem a moment of an individual life, so might a work of art dedicated to the tireless reclamation of a whole vanished world, making it unfold its flowers or houses or people and become permanent and recognizable again. In the living presence of such a work of art, the reader too would be redeemed from the abyss of silence where all things flow into unreality. Such a book would show that we are all treasuries of our own pasts, closed worlds of significance ready to spring open at the skilled touch of an artist's words. In *Time Regained*, the last volume of *Remembrance of Things Past*, Proust looks on the as yet unwritten novel not as a project but as a kind of internal artifact, "something precious and fragile, not belonging to me, which had been confided to my care and which I wanted to hand over intact to those for whom it was destined." Its readers would, ideally, "not be my readers, but the readers of themselves, my book being only a sort of magnifying-glass like those offered by the optician of Combray to a purchaser. So that I should ask neither their praise nor their blame but only that they should tell me if it was right or not, whether the words they were reading within themselves were those I wrote."

Remembrance of Things Past can thus be viewed on one level as an allegory concerning a quest for truth, a quest undertaken to redeem ordinary experience from meaninglessness, to bestow significance on life by giving it the reality and substance of language. Though based on the events of his own life, Proust's work is not offered as an account of what happened to the author. Rather, it is designed to reveal the workings of the individual imagination in its struggle to bring "something which does not exist . . . into the light of day." Such a work of art offers a mental model, so to speak, of a contemporary mind coming to personal terms with ageless problems of meaning.

Just such an artistic purpose links Proust's novel with two autobiographical poems by Dylan Thomas, "Poem in October" and "Fern Hill." In them as in Proust, the artist summons his childhood for scrutiny, in order to comprehend the origins of his creativity and reaffirm its redemptive presence throughout life.

Dylan Thomas was Welsh, born in the small town of Swansea in October 1914; he died at the age of thirty-nine in New York City in an alcoholic coma. He wrote "Poem in October" and "Fern Hill" within two summers of each other, in 1944 and 1945, his last productive years as a poet. After he became famous, Thomas spent much of his life in public, making his living chiefly through reading appearances in person and on BBC radio, all the while collaborating, through acts of public drunkenness and lechery, in the creation of the legend that now embalms him in print. But the details of Thomas's self-destructive public life shed little light on the situations dealt with in his poetry, even in such autobiographical poems as "Poem in October" and "Fern Hill." In these the speaker, though he calls himself "I," represents not a personality but a stage of life. W.H. Auden has described that stage in *The Dyer's Hand,* an account of his own development as a writer: "Between the ages of twenty and forty we are engaged in the process of discovering who we are, which involves learning the difference between accidental limitations which it is our duty to outgrow and the necessary limitations of our nature beyond which we cannot trespass with impunity. Few of us can learn this without making mistakes, without trying to become a little more of the universal man than we are permitted to be."

The Origins of Creativity

At thirty Thomas was not sure whether his talent was capable of further development. World War II, perennial financial difficulties, fear that his creative power was drying up, and persistent ill-health all were part of the climate of limitation in which "Poem in October" and "Fern Hill" were conceived and painfully constructed. (One observer reported seeing over two hundred worksheet revisions of "Fern Hill.") In quest of a former confidence, Thomas returns in the poems, to a period of early childhood when the world seemed one seamless extension of his moods of peace and joy. What he seeks are principles of continuity that might reestablish in the needy present self former capacities of hope and trust.

Poem in October

It was my thirtieth year to heaven
Woke to my hearing from harbour and neighbour wood
And the mussel pooled and the heron
Priested shore
The morning beckon
With water praying and call of seagull and rook
And the knock of sailing boats on the net webbed wall
Myself to set foot
That second
In the still sleeping town and set forth.

My birthday began with the water-
Birds and the birds of the winged trees flying my name
Above the farms and the white horses
And I rose
In rainy autumn
And walked abroad in a shower of all my days.
High tide and the heron dived when I took the road
Over the border
And the gates
Of the town closed as the town awoke.

A springful of larks in a rolling
Cloud and the roadside bushes brimming with whistling
Blackbirds and the sun of October
Summery
On the hill's shoulder,
Here were fond climates and sweet singers suddenly
Come in the morning where I wandered and listened
To the rain wringing
Wind blow cold
In the wood faraway under me.

Pale rain over the dwindling harbour
And over the sea wet church the size of a snail
  With its horns through mist and the castle
     Brown as owls
    But all the gardens
Of spring and summer were blooming in the tall tales
Beyond the border and under the lark full cloud.
    There could I marvel
     My birthday
  Away but the weather turned around.

    It turned away from the blithe country
And down the other air and the blue altered sky
  Streamed again a wonder of summer
      With apples
    Pears and red currants
And I saw in the turning so clearly a child's
Forgotten mornings when he walked with his mother
    Through the parables
     Of sun light
  And the legends of the green chapels

  And the twice told fields of infancy
That his tears burned my cheeks and his heart moved in mine.
  These were the woods the river and sea
     Where a boy
    In the listening
Summertime of the dead whispered the truth of his joy
To the trees and the stones and the fish in the tide.
    And the mystery
     Sang alive
  Still in the water and singingbirds.

  And there could I marvel my birthday
Away but the weather turned around. And the true
  Joy of the long dead child sang burning
     In the sun.
    It was my thirtieth
Year to heaven stood there then in the summer noon
Though the town below lay leaved with October blood.
    O may my heart's truth
     Still be sung
  On this high hill in a year's turning.

A paraphrase of "Poem in October" might go as follows. On his thirtieth birthday, a man takes an early-morning walk to a hill over-looking the town where he grew up. Climbing above a rainstorm, he comes to a sunny patch on the hill, and something he sees stirs a recol-lection; suddenly he is flooded by the memory of walking there in sum-mer, as a child, with his mother. For an instant he is overwhelmed by the past, by the feelings and knowledge he had as a child that now blend with and elevate his adult perceptions. Moved to tears, he prays that this experience will repeat itself in his lifetime.

More than most of Thomas's poetry, "Poem in October" contains a simple story line that gives it a firm structure: beginning, middle, and end. The use of imagery, however, is far from simple. Rarely does Thomas offer figurative language as mere illustration of an abstract concept, in the way, for example, that Robert Burns does in the lines "My love is like a red, red rose / That's newly sprung in June." The justice of Burns's simile lies in its concreteness: the redness, freshness, and evanescence of the rose can be sensed and observed. Imagery in a poem by Thomas is rarely so concrete and verifiable. In stanza five of "Poem in October" Thomas recalls "a child's / Forgotten mornings" with this image:

> he walked with his mother
> Through the parables
> Of sun light.

To unfold the meanings in these lines the reader must collect from the rest of the poem references to light, to childhood, and above all to language and storytelling ("water praying," "birds of the winged trees flying my name," "tall tales / Beyond the border"). Not the natural world but the imaginative world that the poet is building in the poem is the source of coherent meaning for the metaphor "parables / Of sun light"—where, among other meanings, a pun lurks, linking mother and son in the illuminations that parables shed. The story told in "Poem in October" is subsidiary to the main imaginative concerns of the poem; the plot merely supplies a useful framework. The rich explorations in "Poem in October" of the poet's relationship to nature and to his own past take place chiefly at the level of figurative language, in surprising metaphors and brilliant syntactical condensations. As a consequence, in order for the reader to complete with Thomas the journey "beyond the border" that separates the ordinary world from the world suffused by the child's wonder, it is helpful to know something about Thomas's distinctive techniques and goals as a craftsman.

Thomas's Imagery: Let It Breed

One of Thomas's favorite quotations, according to his biographer Paul Ferris, was the opening of the Gospel of John: "In the beginning was the Word." Thomas held that there are only two kinds of poets: those who begin with concepts or objects and end up writing mere descriptions, and those who—like God—begin with words and end up with worlds. Thomas's aesthetic goal throughout life was to avoid intellectuality, objectivity, and any kind of mere descriptiveness. As a consequence he was often criticized for being obscure. He made an eloquent defense of his method of composition in a letter to his friend Henry Treece:

> I make one image—though "make" is not the word; I let, perhaps an image be "made" emotionally in me and then apply to it what intellectual and critical forces I possess—let it breed another, let that image contradict the first, make of the third image bred out of the other two together, a fourth contradictory image, and let them all, within my imposed formal limits, conflict. Each image holds within it the seed of its own destruction, and my dialectal method, as I understand it, is a constant building up and breaking down of the images that come out of the central seed, which is itself destructive and constructive at the same time. . . . Any sequence of my images must be a sequence of creations, recreations, destructions, contradictions.

In "Poem in October" the "central seed" is the story of what the poet did on his birthday, and several kinds of "building up and breaking down of the images" may be observed within the compass of a single line. One particularly rich set of metaphors is initiated in the second line of the poem: "Woke to my hearing from harbour and neighbour wood." "Woke" carries its common meaning in this line: the poem's setting is early morning on the poet's birthday. The poet awakes; then the town awakes, too, once the poet is securely beyond its limits:

> I took the road
> Over the border
> And the gates
> Of the town closed as the town awoke.

But from the outset "woke" signals a symbolic action as well, an action linked with psychological change: the crossing over the border from the

October of computed time to the "summer noon" of recaptured time, from an ordinary to an ecstatic state of consciousness. As the poet woke, so too the inner meaning of his birthday woke—not to his sight (which responds to appearances, to the surface of things) but to his *hearing*, which links him to *heaven*, with the aid of the *heron* (who acts as heaven's earthly mediator, or priest). Heaven beckons him by ear: in the praying of water, the call of seagull and rook, the knock of boats on a net webbed wall. And Thomas courts our comprehension by ear as well, in the numerous internal rhymes and half-rhymes that sing out in these lines: year, shore; heaven, hearing, heron; harbour, neighbour; heron, beckon, second; mussel, call, seagull, wall; woke, rook, knock; foot, forth. Thomas seems in fact to have been careful in this stanza to avoid imagery that is concretely visual. It is difficult, for example, to make visual sense of such statements as "the morning beckon" or "water praying." Even "the net webbed wall" supplies greater auditory precision to the sound the boats make. Hearing, not sight, is the dominant sense throughout "Poem in October" because hearing is a path by which imaginative truth reaches us, via story and song, all our lives, perhaps especially during childhood. This is why, when Thomas has fully recrossed the border separating manhood from childhood, he finds a mother walking a child "through the *parables* / Of sun light / And the *legends* of the green chapels / And the *twice told fields* of infancy" (italics added) while the memory culminates in a recovery of the power to *hear* "the true / Joy of the long dead child" and to *sing* that same heart's truth again.

Another set of metaphors is bred from the second half of the line: "Woke to my hearing from harbour and neighbour wood." A polarity between the harbor from which the poet sets out and the hill to which he climbs is established immediately. As the poem develops, movement from present to past is reflected in a gradual change in the source of imagery, from water to garden. Water, through its associations with time and change in the poem, is contrasted with the stability of a certain memory: a childhood scene lit by eternal sunlight, an earthly paradise. This birthday is a *rebirth*-day, and Thomas is summoned to it by flowing water, falling water:

> I rose
> In rainy autumn
> And walked abroad in a shower of all my days.

Water praying, water birds flying his name, a springful of larks, and bushes brimming with blackbirds all assist in converting the solid ground of ordinary life into a fluid context for the dissolving of present into past, man into child, common into holy. The poem is drenched with the sight and sound of moving water until stanza five, where the weather turns around, and "streamed" denotes the flow of wonder, like sunlight, illuminating a place fixed in memory:

> And down the other air and the blue altered sky
> Streamed again a wonder of summer
> With apples
> Pears and red currants
> And I saw in the turning so clearly a child's
> Forgotten mornings when he walked with his mother.

As a consequence of Thomas's technique of composition—letting images breed, producing "a sequence of creations, recreations, destructions, contradictions"—any of his poems, including "Poem in October," contains elements impossible to integrate with a paraphrase of the story line. A single reading—even better, a single hearing—illustrates this. "Poem in October" is Thomas at his best. His use of language is so arresting, musical, vital, and, finally, sacramental that his poetry usually appeals to readers at once—especially if they are listening to his recorded readings of it—whether or not they are following his meaning. Thomas's poetry opens what the Anglo-Saxons called our "word-hoard," the large coffers of our language (of which our personal use is likely to be paltry in daily life). Nonetheless, "Poem in October" does have a theme similar to that of the passage from Proust discussed earlier: the joy of childhood, symbolic of the poet's original creative power, and the recapturing of that joy, symbolic of the renewing of that creative power.

The Child as Symbol

Thomas ends his birthday poem with a prayer that he may sustain the vision into which he has been reborn that day:

> And the true
> Joy of the long dead child sang burning
> In the sun.
> It was my thirtieth
> Year to heaven stood there then in the summer noon
> Though the town below lay leaved with October blood.
> O may my heart's truth
> Still be sung
> On this high hill in a year's turning.

If we are not too enchanted by Thomas's lovely rhetoric, we might as adults stop here to question the implication of these last lines, the idea that his birthday windfall of momentary escape into the happier past might actually have some significance for the future. To understand this hope, we must understand the meaning Thomas associates with "the long dead child" who has been temporarily revitalized in the living man. The boy in "Poem in October" is not simply young Dylan Marlais Thomas. He is, rather, the Child: a human being at an early stage of cognitive development, a mind that has not fully developed the powers of reason and still maintains a "primal sympathy" with nature.

Primal sympathy is a term from William Wordsworth's "Ode: Intimations of Immortality from Recollections of Early Childhood," which directly or indirectly influenced the composition of "Poem in October." Wordsworth's poem opens with a prayer very like the one that ends Thomas's:

> The Child is father of the Man;
> And I could wish my days to be
> Bound each to each by natural piety.

Wordsworth worked on this poem for two years (he was thirty-four when he finished it), during a period of intense creative activity. He was attempting to write a great epic for his time but was often discouraged by his sense of personal limitation, both "accidental" and "necessary," to recall Auden's distinction. As the epigraph to the Ode indicates, Wordsworth is trying in this poem to dismiss as accidental—that is, as reversible—the habits of perception that deaden the adult mind, and to reclaim the intuitive powers he recalls having had in childhood: "I could wish my days to be / Bound each to each."

Despite its title, Wordsworth's Ode has little to do with immortality. Rather, it is concerned with two contrary states of perception, one native to childhood, the other to mental habits acquired in the course of growing up. The poem opens in a mood of grief, with a statement of loss:

There was a time when meadow, grove, and stream
The earth, and every common sight,
    To me did seem
    Appareled in celestial light,
The glory and the freshness of a dream.
It is not now as it hath been of yore—
    Turn whereso'er I may,
      By night or day,
The things which I have seen I now can see no more.

    The Rainbow comes and goes,
    And lovely is the Rose,
    The Moon doth with delight
Look round her when the heavens are bare;
    Waters on a starry night
    Are beautiful and fair;
   The sunshine is a glorious birth;
   But yet I know, where'er I go,
That there hath passed away a glory from the earth.

As in "Poem in October" the poet's reconnection with the lost child in himself is not the result of intellectual effort; it occurs involuntarily, as a rift in consciousness, a breakthrough as sudden as a change in the weather or a shift of wind that enlivens a fire:

    O joy! that in our embers
    Is something that doth live,
    That nature yet remembers
    What was so fugitive!
The thought of our past years in me doth breed
Perpetual benediction: . . .
. . . .
    . . . for those first affections,
    Those shadowy recollections,
    Which, be they what they may,
Are yet the fountain light of all our day,
Are yet a master light of all our seeing.

Wordsworth's mood has turned from sorrow to joy on the pivot of an insight: the perception of "glory," which was his only mode of sight in early childhood, has not vanished but is merely fugitive. The "first affections" felt for the world still remain. The original power of perception, which he calls "primal sympathy," has not been lost at all; Wordsworth has discovered its place in an ongoing and inclusive process: "those first affections . . . / Are *yet* the fountain light of all our day, / Are *yet* a master light of all our seeing" (italics added). Light, the fugitive visionary gleam from the opening of the Ode, returns to the poem in this metaphor of "fountain light," fanned into life out of embers, and closes the stanza with a resolving image in which water and light, hearing and vision, coalesce:

> Hence in a season of calm weather
> Though inland far we be,
> Our Souls have sight of that immortal sea
> Which brought us hither,
> Can in a moment travel thither,
> And see the Children sport upon the shore,
> And hear the mighty waters rolling evermore.

Chronology—the logic of time—vanishes. The mind withdraws from time into space. Within it, Child and Man are contained simultaneously, "bound each to each," fulfilling the wish in the earliest lines of the poem. Stationed on the shore midway between Man and sea, between present and eternity, the Child does not return the gaze of the Man nor does he comprehend the rolling of the mighty waters as the music of time. Yet the Child has been recovered by the Man, once and for all, within the boundaries of an inner space—in the form of an intuitive confidence that Child and Man are not separate entities but stages in a process of development, each stage incorporating and building upon the last. This mature vision, which allows the poet to see and know himself in the context of time, has been attained at the cost of growing up. But the poem moves toward its ending in a mood of peace:

> Though nothing can bring back the hour
> Of splendor in the grass, of glory in the flower;
> We will grieve not, rather find
> Strength in what remains behind;
> In the primal sympathy
> Which having been must ever be.

The restoration of an inner Child accessible now and then during certain seasons in the weather of the soul is, I think, the same reunion celebrated in "Poem in October":

the weather turned around. And the true
Joy of the long dead child sang burning
In the sun.
It was my thirtieth
Year to heaven stood there then in the summer noon
Though the town below lay leaved with October blood.

Because of the verbal echoes, it is possible that Thomas had Wordsworth's Ode consciously in mind when writing "Poem in October." Whether he did or not, Thomas was obviously writing under the influence of a belief about the psychology of the poet's art that Wordsworth— with the help of Samuel Taylor Coleridge—initially formulated, and that poets as well as developmental psychologists still hold. Wordsworth and Coleridge believed that the highest human faculty was not the power of reason ("discursive understanding," as Coleridge called it) but of imagination. Eighteenth-century rationalists had viewed the processes of thought as almost mechanical: the mind, in the words of John Locke, was "a blank tablet, void of all characters" until painted by experience; the mind arrived at truth by generalizing from experience. Art in this period was thought of as "invention," poetry as "a mirror held up to nature," which reflected existing realities and passed judgment on them from a position of moral authority. Alexander Pope and Samuel Johnson, whose poems bore such titles as "Essay on Man" and "The Vanity of Human Wishes," were two of the most honored poets of the period.

In opposition to this mechanistic model of the mind, Coleridge, writing in *The Statesman's Manual* in the early nineteenth century, followed Kant and other revolutionary German philosophers in describing the mind as radically creative. Above "discursive understanding," which Coleridge describes as knowledge arriving in the form of generalities and abstract categories, he places "Imagination"—"that reconciling and mediatory power" which works by "*incorporating* the reason in images of the sense and . . . gives birth to a system of symbols, harmonious in themselves, and consubstantial with the truths of which they are the conductors." The body metaphors Coleridge uses ("incorporating" and "consubstantial") convey his belief that the ground of knowledge is the whole human being: every nerve, every cell, as well as each organ of sense, presumably plays a role in perception.

Coleridge's insistence on imagination as an avenue to knowledge arises from the observation that some forms of thinking are nondiscursive, nonlinear, and do not result in generalizations; their fruit is the poetic symbol. And in the work of both Wordsworth and Thomas, the child is the symbol for that intuitive form of thought in its earliest manifestations. Because prerational, animistic generosity is the nature of the human mind's first way of knowing, it remains, Wordsworth writes, a capacity "which having been, must ever be." In "Poem in October" Thomas characterizes that child-mind in metaphors of listening and singing:

> a boy
> In the listening
> Summertime of the dead whispered the truth of his joy
> To the trees and the stones and the fish in the tide.
> And the mystery
> Sang alive
> Still in the water and singingbirds.
> . . . .
> O may my heart's truth
> Still be sung. . . .

Whereas for Wordsworth the Child is purely a condition of active *vision,* for Thomas he is a condition of active *voice.* Thomas hopes to reclaim for himself the intuitive power by which things reveal themselves as symbols, without the intervention of reason and abstraction. Thus he describes the child as inhabiting a world already infused with language ("parables of sunlight," "legends of green chapels," "twice told fields of infancy"). The adult Thomas crosses the border into this heaven-appointed state as into a garden of "tall tales," after waking to hear nature beckon him, "flying my *name* / Above the farms" (italics added).

This state of imaginative consciousness for both Thomas and Wordsworth is the expression of the divine in the human. In the last stanza of "Poem in October," an apocalyptic figure stands revealed in the summer noon. The town below belongs to time, but the man who has become "as a little child again" belongs for an instant to the kingdom of heaven. The biblical references are unmistakable, yet the poem pulls no boxcar of footnotes. The Book of Revelations has become merely the book of nature, opening its meanings without mediation to the vexed heart of a human being in need of truth.

The Sanctity of the Past

The same cunningly simple use of religious tradition to enlarge the scope of his personal theme appears in Thomas's other poem about his childhood, "Fern Hill." This poem might be called a realization of the story, in the Book of Genesis, of Adam in Paradise, a recreation of that story in terms of the poet's own lost childhood.

Fern Hill

Now as I was young and easy under the apple boughs
About the lilting house and happy as the grass was green,
    The night above the dingle starry,
        Time let me hail and climb
      Golden in the heydays of his eyes,
And honoured among wagons I was prince of the apple towns
And once below a time I lordly had the trees and leaves
        Trail with daisies and barley
    Down the rivers of the windfall light.

And as I was green and carefree, famous among the barns
About the happy yard and singing as the farm was home,
    In the sun that is young once only,
        Time let me play and be
      Golden in the mercy of his means,
And green and golden I was huntsman and herdsman, the calves
Sang to my horn, the foxes on the hills barked clear and cold,
        And the sabbath rang slowly
    In the pebbles of the holy streams.

All the sun long it was running, it was lovely, the hay
Fields high as the house, the tunes from the chimneys, it was air
    And playing, lovely and watery
        And fire green as grass.
    And nightly under the simple stars
As I rode to sleep the owls were bearing the farm away,
All the moon long I heard, blessed among stables, the night-jars
        Flying with the ricks, and the horses
          Flashing into the dark.

And then to awake, and the farm, like a wanderer white
With the dew, come back, the cock on his shoulder: it was all
      Shining, it was Adam and maiden,
          The sky gathered again
      And the sun grew round that very day.
So it must have been after the birth of the simple light
In the first, spinning place, the spellbound horses walking warm
      Out of the whinnying green stable
          On to the fields of praise.

And honoured among foxes and pheasants by the gay house
Under the new made clouds and happy as the heart was long,
      In the sun born over and over,
          I ran my heedless ways,
      My wishes raced through the house high hay
And nothing I cared, at my sky blue trades, that time allows
In all his tuneful turning so few and such morning songs
      Before the children green and golden
          Follow him out of grace,

Nothing I cared, in the lamb white days, that time would take me
Up to the swallow thronged loft by the shadow of my hand,
      In the moon that is always rising,
          Nor that riding to sleep
      I should hear him fly with the high fields
And wake to the farm forever fled from the childless land.
Oh as I was young and easy in the mercy of his means,
          Time held me green and dying
      Though I sang in my chains like the sea.

Fernhill Farm was a place belonging to Thomas's aunt, which he visited frequently during the summer as a child. Because he was reared by a mother devout in the practice of Welsh nonconformist Protestantism, Thomas's early years probably contained a good deal of Sunday school. Idyllic summer memories fuse easily with references to Paradise in "Fern Hill," as if the two had been indistinguishable in his early mind, and equally real. As an adult, however, the poet has specific designs on his childhood; he is here explaining to himself the feeling of sanctity that carries over from the past. The aspects of Genesis that interest Thomas in this poem—what Eden was like, and what it means to have fallen from innocence—interest him not as a scholar or theologian but as an adult turning to the past in order to understand himself better in the present.

The Child as Adam

Thomas does not rewrite the act of Creation as it is narrated in Genesis; the Edenic farm is luminously complete at the opening of "Fern Hill." Rather, Thomas takes up the story on the sixth day, after the creation of Adam, when God has set him in the garden to till it and keep it, giving Adam dominion over every living thing.

Adam's dominion over creation is the particular theme of the first two stanzas of "Fern Hill." Eve does not figure in this garden, except through a single reference ("it was all / Shining, it was Adam and maiden"). Adam is its sole lord, and the apple boughs are merely another particular in God's plenty. Thomas loads these lines with honorifics: the child is "honoured," a "prince," "lordly," "famous" among the other creatures. The child's "work" is a paradisal version of labor. While the adults presumably till the fields on Fernhill Farm, the child takes charge of letting the trees grow: "I lordly had the trees and leaves / Trail with daisies and barley." He is herdsman of calves, huntsman of the fox's bark.

Attributing actions to the child, however, ignores an important element built into the poem through careful use of verbs. The first four stanzas exude energy, all associated with the child. But with few exceptions, the child is, grammatically, the subject of no active verbs. He does not *do*, but simply *is*. "Hail," "climb," "play," "rode (to sleep)," and "heard" are the only exceptions. By far the greatest number of verbs for which the child is the subject ascribe existence rather than action: "I was." Even the exuberant activities described in the third stanza are displaced from the child: "it was running . . . / . . . it was air / And playing." The action is abstract, as in a still photograph. For Paradise in "Fern Hill" is a vibrant stasis, motion without consequence, diversity without process. Even night and day are not stages, but alternating states of light. The stars appear (and they are "simple stars," for the child knows nothing about the fates they rule), the farm is borne away for a while, and then "like a wanderer white / With the dew, come[s] back, the cock on his shoulder"—unchanged; the sun is "born over and over."

So it must have been, the poet muses in stanza four, in the newly created Eden. Thomas's vision of the "horses walking warm / . . . On to the fields of praise" owes little to Genesis ("out of the ground the Lord God formed every beast of the field"), but Thomas does appear to owe something to Milton, whose account in *Paradise Lost* (Book VII) of the creation of the animals has the same delightful concreteness:

Among the Trees in Pairs they rose, they walk'd:
The Cattle in the Fields and Meadows green,
Those rare and solitary, these in flocks
Pasturing at once, and in broad Herds upsprung.
The grassy Clods now Calv'd, now half appear'd
The Tawny Lion, pawing to get free
His hinder parts, then springs as broke from Bonds
And Rampant shakes his Brinded mane; the Ounce
The Libbard, and the Tiger, as the Mole
Rising, the crumbl'd Earth above them threw
In Hillocks; the swift Stag from under ground
Bore up his branching head.

Thomas imagines the horses rising full-grown and warm out of the mind of the Creator, still spellbound from being spun into existence by a command:

So it must have been after the birth of the simple light
In the first, spinning place, the spellbound horses walking warm
Out of the whinnying green stable
On to the fields of praise.

Paradise, then, is the state of changeless happiness in "Fern Hill." Yet from the first stanza, Time, personified, is a presence in the garden. And just as the child's portrayal identifies him with Adam, so Time's actions identify him with the progenitor of Creation. The Book of Genesis suggests that God took great pleasure in Eden: he "saw everything that He had made, and behold, it was very good"; he wondered what Adam would name the animals; he walked in the garden in the cool of the day. The figure of Time in "Fern Hill" seems to be an extrapolation from these details, a parent who delights in the exercise of benevolence: "Time let me hail and climb"; "Time let me play and be." We may recall that God's first word in the English Bible is "let" ("Let there be light, and it was so"). In Genesis, of course, "Let" is a command: the mode of God's intrusion on chaos with his creative will. Thomas applies this word to Time in its other sense: "to permit." Time's fatherly permissiveness is the child's source of grace: "Time let me play and be / Golden in the mercy of his means"—like Adam in Eden before his fall. Paradoxically, then, Time himself is the guardian of the fragile equilibrium that keeps Paradise in existence.

In this reading of "Fern Hill" I have thus far been describing the story elements in the poem at the expense of attention to Thomas's craft. Though the story may be discerned within the poem as a structure, as in "Poem in October," another type of patterning is achieved through repetition of imagery. In "Fern Hill" we can watch Thomas "breed," as he says, the images of things green and the images of things golden, generating a "sequence of creations, recreations, destructions, contradictions."

"Green" occurs seven times in "Fern Hill," "golden" four times; twice they are yoked, "green and golden." Green usually connotes the condition of being very young, like new grass (stanza one). In stanza two, green is the energy of the carefree, famous, singing huntsman-herdsman child; it is also the freshness and wonder of all young beings, both child and world (i.e., the "green stable" at the world's beginning). Youth is a state of "green" also in the sense of unknowing: the child is "green and carefree" because he cared "Nothing . . . that time would take me"; he was "heedless" of time. Most significantly, the child's happiness is called green "as grass." Echoing the Biblical lament, "All flesh is grass," in linking the child's joy to an ephemeral natural thing, Thomas implies the child's mortality from the opening lines. (Recall Thomas's statement about his method: "Each image holds within it the seed of its own destruction.") But this meaning of green remains only latent in the imagery until the beautiful last lines: "Time held me green and dying / Though I sang in my chains like the sea." Green is a stage in the process of dying, just as grass is a stage of hay.

"Golden," on the other hand, signifies only one thing: blessedness. It is linked to the green that signifies wonder, freshness, and energy. It is likened to a certain temporary stage in the processes of nature—the paradisal stage, wherein the child is still a "prince" and "lordly" among the fields and creatures and is in a certain sense unconscious, "happy as the grass." To be golden is a condition of grace that Time permits out of mercy for the green being: ("Time let me hail and climb / Golden"; "Time let me play and be / Golden"). In the last stanza the child, no longer "easy in the mercy of his means," is also no longer golden—only "green and dying." Many other progeny emerge from this breeding of green and golden. Hay, for example, is green when in the fields (in its "heydays," stanza one) but presumably golden when piled in the ricks of stanza four.

Thomas also breeds new meanings by reworking familiar formulas, exploding clichés by making surprising substitutions: "once below a time," "happy as the grass was green," "singing as the farm was home," "happy as the heart was long." This is a sly way to compel attention. The familiar phrase is "once upon a time," so why "below"? Is it because Time in "Fern Hill" looms over this "prince of the apple towns" as God looms over Adam in Eden? Or that as children we begin "carefree" and "heedless," which is in a sense below the consciousness we gradually grow "up" to attain?

The Artist as Guardian

This question brings me finally to the theme Thomas's poems share with Proust's novel: the relation of adult to child as symbolic of the relation of artist to society. For though "Fern Hill" is a poem about Adam in Eden, in the ways I have described, Thomas has adapted the story in order to explore a truth implicit in the realities of human experience. Genesis is particularly useful to Thomas not only because of its spare design and colorful details, but also because of its cultural authority. Most of us hear the story of Genesis before we hear of Darwin. Yet God and Adam and Eden are themselves symbols abstracted from a compelling and problematic fact about human existence: all children live in a protected world dominated by parents who are in every way bigger than they. The parent is not only the source of one's own existence but the personification of tradition. The parent's "Yes" and "No" transmit to the child a world already fully shaped long before the child appeared in it. And the first human task, as "Fern Hill" so lovingly paints it, is that of *acceptance* of the world through every portal of sense, every faculty (Thomas uses the word "hail": to greet, to welcome).

Childhood's end comes with the gradual recognition that this is not a world of vibrant stasis but of change, and more important, of choice. The development of this consciousness sentences the child to the loss of every illusion. Thus in "Fern Hill," Time absconds with the fields of Paradise ("I . . . hear him fly with the high fields / And wake to the farm forever fled from the childless land"), abandoning the child as irretrievably as Adam was shut out from Eden by the angel with the flaming sword.

In both stories, the cause of this change is the acquisition of consciousness. Condemning Adam to the world as we know it, God says, "the man has become like one of us, knowing good and evil." God, then, is not merely one's parent, but—what is more sobering—he is the same doomed kind of being as oneself: "the children green and golden / Follow him out of grace." But it is also this parent figure in "Fern Hill" who *leads* the child, in a movement of ascent to knowledge, "Up to the swallow thronged loft by the shadow of my hand / In the moon that is always rising." Recognition of the shadow of one's hand, particularly by the reflected light of the ever-changing moon, is emblematic both of one's mortality and of one's power. The hand of the writer shapes a human shadow that imprints the void with meanings.

I am suggesting, then, that "Fern Hill" is structured by a myth and by a psychological realism, both of which trace consciousness from its primary stage of innocence—the unknowingness of childhood—to the threshold of creative responsibility. Genesis, refracted through Thomas's imagination in "Fern Hill," becomes a myth about consciousness: about its origins in the divine will to distinguish man from the rest of creation on the basis of his power to know and name the world; and about the necessity of each person's entrance, through consciousness, into history, where all of us must come to understand our own being in the context of time, process, and change. The gift that Adam bears out of Eden is to be, like God, the author of himself. Hence the poet-consciousness in "Fern Hill" as in other modern poems is to some extent a shadowy image of God in Genesis—an author making a world from the position of comprehension and handing it on to the generations, who will need a guide as they follow him out of grace.

This aspect of the symbol of Time reflects Thomas's sense of the poet's legacy of responsibility. In "Fern Hill," Time is not a concept. He is a human figure big enough to hold a child in his arms and wise enough to show mercy. He is an adult who shares the child's mortality and takes responsibility for leading children out of grace into knowledge. He is, in fact, the prototype of the artist viewed earlier in Proust—in the roles of teacher and father—a guardian. As a personification of this caring function, "Time" is a better name than "Father" or "I"; it conveys the generalized responsibility of the older generation for the younger, and the myriad relationships in which that responsibility is expressed and fulfilled.

Dylan Thomas presents the artist as guardian in both poems dealing with his childhood. His backward gaze is elegiac, yet it evokes an emotion more significant than nostalgia. The weakness inherent in the elegiac mode is that it celebrates something "forever fled" and all the more precious for being irretrievable. But precisely because the "I" Thomas writes about so formally is not merely himself but Child and Man "bound each to each," these poems transcend the limitations of nostalgia. "Poem in October" and "Fern Hill" voice the poet's recognition of himself as bound in the chains of time, a continuum embracing the past yet bearing him steadily into the future—a void he must fill with his comprehending song.

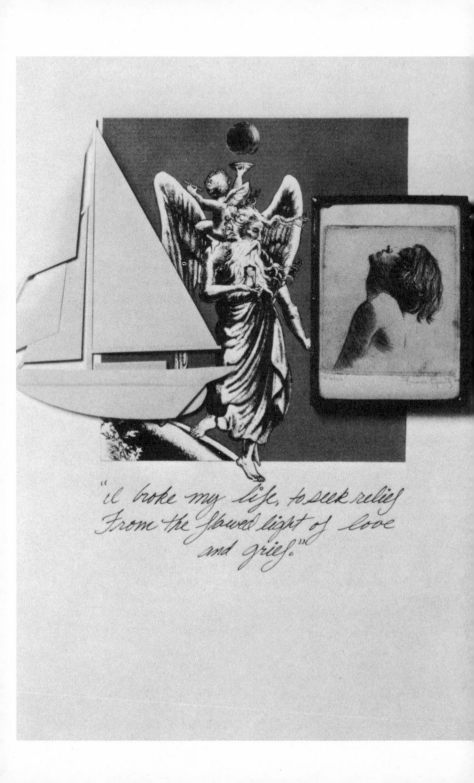

"il broke my life, to seek relief
From the flawed light of love
and grief."

CHAPTER THREE

Liberation:
Poetry of William Butler Yeats
and Louise Bogan

The body is a poor vessel for transcendence.
Elizabeth Hardwick, from "Domestic Manners"

KENNETH BURKE IN *Language as Symbolic Action* defines man as "characteristically the symbol-using animal" and goes on to clarify: "Just as a bird presumably likes to fly or a fish to swim . . . we humans might like to exercise our prowess with symbol systems just because that's the kind of animal we are." The power to make symbols is indeed the trait that distinguishes humans from other forms of life. Exercising our prowess in symbolic action—remembering the past, projecting the future, abstracting ideas from experience—we liberate ourselves from the constraints of sheerly physical existence. Unlike the body, the mind is free to roam in realms of possibility, and it takes delight in the sheer exercise of this power. A short story by James McConkey, entitled "The Idea of Hawk" describes the joy of that experience:

> One likes the idea, say, of *hawk,* and would aspire to it: the
> high freedom, the swift and effortless flight, the sharpness of
> eye, the vertical dive. For example, on a sunny day last spring,
> my wife and I, after planting our garden, lay on our backs in

the grass, enjoying the warmth of the damp soil and the movement of a hawk far above us as it banked and climbed in the updraft. It became a dark point, a mote swimming with the others in the pools of our sun-blinded vision, and then it plunged. As it fell (for a moment I thought we were its prey), crows, those keen-sighted but heavier birds, slowly rose from various positions along the border of the woods that half encircled the horizon. The hawk was the tip of a diminishing stamen, the crows the end points of petals folding back upon the pistil. Hawk and crows composed a blossom so exquisite and inevitable in its movement toward enclosure that I felt the ache to be stamen or petal or—most crucial of all—seed of that pistil. But who in his normal mind would want to be hawk settling down with talons outspread to rake a tiny mouse, to be bird of carrion after a bit of pink intestine? (*The New Yorker Magazine,* June 26, 1978)

In this paragraph, ideal and actual are as beautifully balanced as the hawk in its element. On the side of the actual are man and wife at rest after a day's labor, the warmth and dampness of the soil beneath their backs, and the density of the woods, which makes a clear line defining the horizon. Within these established limits the birds blossom into a symbol. Aided by eyes that are, significantly, half-blinded, the imagination traces in the hawk's flight and the crows' disturbance a pattern like the tracery that at night connects points of light into constellations. The resulting image of the hawk-blossom is the perfect incarnation of a self-ideal expressing freedom and control; the narrator's mind closes on it with an ache of recognition and longing. However, it is an identity formed one instant to be abandoned the next, when the "normal mind" returns, restoring the perspective of actuality, even insisting on the ugliest alternative it can truthfully offer to the idea of hawk.

At certain times, lasting gains can be achieved in such flights of imagination. Particularly during periods of stress caused by depression or by changes over which the individual has no control, the mind is often at work composing and demolishing self-imagery that floats to the surface of consciousness because the human being needs it to reacquire confidence that life has meaning. In realms of symbolic action—dreams, fantasies, interior monologues—the self explores its own capacities for growth and change.

Renewal of the sense of possibility and of inner wholeness is the theme of two very different poems I shall discuss in this chapter. "Sailing to Byzantium," by William Butler Yeats, is about a man's desire to escape from the humiliations of aging. "The Alchemist," by Louise Bogan, is about the desire to attain spiritual authority through denial of the flesh. In both poems the impure, intractable, and mortal human body becomes the symbol for everything that stands in the way of desire. And yet both poets, in accepting the limitations imposed on desire by reality, win the truest freedom: the liberation of the mind from obsession and illusion, thus from anguish that is largely self-imposed.

The Transformation of Desire: William Butler Yeats's "Sailing to Byzantium"

Writing poetry is a profession in which age seems to influence performance very little. Youthful poets have written poems of overwhelming intellectual authority and artistic skill; the examples of Rimbaud and Keats come immediately to mind. On the other hand, some poets attain full mastery of their talent late in life. Both Wallace Stevens and Robert Penn Warren wrote most of the pages in their volumes of collected poems after the age of sixty. William Butler Yeats (1863-1939) is one of the few poets whose careers include the extremes of significant artistic achievement both early and late in life. He published his first poems when he was twenty-two and wrote his last poems on his deathbed at seventy-six. Although Yeats's intellectual preoccupations viewed in retrospect seem to have remained consistent, his artistic strategies in exploring them changed radically every ten to fifteen years. The best developed near the last, when among other topics Yeats wrote in tones of stringent candor about aging—particularly his longing for a further development of creative power before death or senility took away his cultivated mastery of his craft.

Art as a Path to Truth

Yeats was Irish, born into a circle of artists both living and dead. His entire life was dominated by art. John Butler Yeats, his father, was a painter who moved his family to London when William was twenty in order to work among the Pre-Raphaelites, the painters of the day he most admired. Artists Dante Gabriel Rossetti, Edward Burne-Jones, and James A. McNeill Whistler and writers Oscar Wilde and William Morris were among friends accessible to the young Yeats in his earliest years as an aspiring poet. During his childhood his father tirelessly introduced aesthetics into every aspect of the family's daily life. Yeats recalled that his father was fond of reading the most passionate scenes from Shakespeare at the breakfast table.

As Yeats matured, art played a role in his life analogous to that of religion in the lives of some people. Yeats saw aesthetic form as the means by which an eternal spirit manifested itself in the material world in ever-changing forms. Yeats wrote continuously of the transactions between the individual artist and the spiritual tradition that was the source of the artist's truth, formulating in *A Vision,* an occult prose work, an entire philosophical system based on a view of history as cyclical. Yeats tried to keep his work highly integrated: he intended in *A Vision* to clarify the ideas latent in the poetry, and he carefully organized his individual books of poems so that each poem took its place in an orderly—usually dialectical—development of thought and feeling. "One poem lights up another," he asserted. "Sailing to Byzantium" is a poem that reflects Yeats's belief system and his esoteric studies; yet it can be fully understood without reference to his other work as a poem about the hatred of growing old and the longing to attain a different kind of passionate intensity and integrity from that of youth.

Sailing to Byzantium

I

That is no country for old men. The young
In one another's arms, birds in the trees
—Those dying generations—at their song,
The salmon-falls, the mackerel-crowded seas,
Fish, flesh, or fowl, commend all summer long
Whatever is begotten, born, and dies.
Caught in that sensual music all neglect
Monuments of unaging intellect.

II

An aged man is but a paltry thing,
A tattered coat upon a stick, unless
Soul clap its hands and sing, and louder sing
For every tatter in its mortal dress,
Nor is there singing school but studying
Monuments of its own magnificence;
And therefore I have sailed the seas and come
To the holy city of Byzantium.

III

O sages standing in God's holy fire
As in the gold mosaic of a wall,
Come from the holy fire, perne in a gyre,
And be the singing-masters of my soul.
Consume my heart away; sick with desire
And fastened to a dying animal
It knows not what it is; and gather me
Into the artifice of eternity.

IV

Once out of nature I shall never take
My bodily form from any natural thing,
But such a form as Grecian goldsmiths make
Of hammered gold and gold enameling
To keep a drowsy Emperor awake;
Or set upon a golden bough to sing
To lords and ladies of Byzantium
Of what is past, or passing, or to come.

The emotional center of "Sailing to Byzantium" is the poet's prayer to the sages in stanza III:

> Consume my heart away; sick with desire
> And fastened to a dying animal
> It knows not what it is; and gather me
> Into the artifice of eternity.

Yeats said in a letter to a friend written about the time he composed "Sailing to Byzantium" that he aspired, as an old man, to write poems befitting his age, poems of "joy in the passing moment, emotion without the bitterness of memory." Clearly, "Sailing to Byzantium" is dominated by no such stereotype of noble old age. Nor need one be old to have felt the emotion expressed in this stanza, a blending of physical disgust, like Hamlet's repugnance of being "too, too sullied flesh," and of envy for the apparently mindless eroticism of everyone else. The deliverance Yeats seems to envision is a poetic sleight of hand whereby the mortal being is transformed painlessly into one of the "monuments of unaging intellect"—an artistic goal like that of Shakespeare in the many sonnets in which the poet, contemplating the effects of time, consoles himself with the thought that his art can perpetuate the beauty of a "dying animal" in a form more lasting than flesh:

> . . . Time that gave doth now his gift confound.
> Time doth transfix the flourish set on youth
> And delves the parallels in beauty's brow,
> Feeds on the rarities of nature's truth,
> And nothing stands but for his scythe to mow:
> And yet to times in hope my verse shall stand,
> Praising thy worth, despite his cruel hand.
>
> —from Sonnet 60

Yeats's lyric, like Shakespeare's sonnets on this theme, contains a buried linear argument: mortal, I desire to be somehow immortal, and will be when I have converted my passions into poems. The poet's hope is fulfilled each time a reader completes the creation undertaken in the poem, bringing back the poet's thought from the "artifice of eternity" Yeats seeks in stanza III. But such long-deferred and posthumously conferred satisfaction does not seem an adequate cure for a person "sick with desire." Indeed "Sailing to Byzantium" contains a self-affirmation richer and more ambiguous than confidence in a posthumous reward. To comprehend this self-affirmation one must for a moment ignore Yeats's conclusions in order to reflect on his contradictions.

The Defeat of Envy

"Sailing to Byzantium" is structurally composed of sets of paired opposites—dominated by conceptual polarities expressed in the rhymes of eter*nity* versus *me*; *art*ifice versus *heart*. On the side of heart (and opposed to artifice) are live birds in the trees (versus a golden bird on a golden bough); sensual music (versus the soul's song); the fecund diversity of the natural world, "the salmon-falls, the mackerel-crowded seas" (versus the patterned diversity of unchanging art, "the gold mosaic of a wall"); "that country" (versus "Byzantium"). Though complementary, the realm of heart and the realm of artifice occupy different territory; one belongs to passing time, the other to the agelessness of works of art.

The narrator of the poem, an old man, feels rejected by the world that the young occupy with mindless joy. "Sailing to Byzantium" is, I think, not so much a poem about the desire to transcend the aging body as about the desire to transcend the state of bitter envy with which the poem opens. Envy is deadly to the vitality of imagination, because it is both obsessive and ungenerous. More important, envy involves exercise of the will in an effort to achieve what cannot be achieved by will. One cannot will fulfillment through sensuality, for sensual appetite is by nature insatiable, inevitably recurring; neither can one will one's appeal to others as an object of sexual desire. Yet in the first stanza the poet appears to wish he could do both. I hear a tone of painful chagrin at exclusion from the happier lot of others in his opening phrase, "That is no country for old men," and in the contemptuous denouncements that follow: "the young in one another's arms," "those dying generations . . . / . . . caught in that sensual music." Obsessed by lust, an aged man can come to seem to himself worthless, "a paltry thing / A tattered coat upon a stick."

The bitter feelings of sexual rejection expressed in "Sailing to Byzantium" are unusual in Yeats's work. Yeats wrote a good deal of erotic poetry late in life. At fifty-four he married for the first time, and much of his poetry from then on revels in the delight of sexual discovery. In his erotic poems, sensuality is frequently treated as a path to revelation, sexual consummation as an expression of the unity that binds every living thing in the wheel of eternity. This perception forms the wisdom of Yeats's character Crazy Jane, who, when a bishop tries to instruct her on spiritual matters, replies:

> "Fair and foul are near of kin,
> And fair needs foul," I cried.
> "My friends are gone, but that's a truth
> Nor grave nor bed denied,
> Learned in bodily lowliness
> And in the heart's pride.
>
> "A woman can be proud and stiff
> When on love intent;
> But Love has pitched his mansion in
> The place of excrement;
> For nothing can be sole or whole
> That has not been rent."

In "Sailing to Byzantium," then, the repudiation of the "sensual music" of stanza I can be seen as a metaphor for the rejection of seductions— sexual and otherwise—that tempt the artist from the practice of his calling. The poet abandons a desire that cannot be fulfilled by the will

for one that can. The man "sick with desire" can thus be understood as seeking a consummation beyond the temporary satisfaction of sexual climax, a meaning that enters the poem in stanza II:

> An aged man is but a paltry thing,
> A tattered coat upon a stick, unless
> Soul clap its hands and sing, and louder sing
> For every tatter in its mortal dress,
> Nor is there singing school but studying
> Monuments of its own magnificence;
> And therefore I have sailed the seas and come
> To the holy city of Byzantium.

In hoping for the transformation of the aged man into a singing soul, Yeats is not seeking an escape from physical life. Rather he is seeking instruction. The ravages of his flesh cannot be undone, but he can turn his scars into the poetry of personal experience, teaching his soul to sing louder because of every tatter. T.S. Eliot remarked admiringly in his essay "Yeats" that the greatest of Yeats's poetry was the late, highly biographical poetry in which he achieved an unusual impersonality: that of the poet "who, out of intense and personal experience, is able to express a general truth; retaining all the particularity of his experience, to make of it a general symbol. . . . It is not that he became a different man, for . . . one feels sure that the intense experience of youth had been lived through—and indeed, without this early experience he could never have attained anything of the wisdom which appears in his later writing. But he had to wait for a later maturity to find expression of early experience; and this makes him, I think, a unique and especially interesting poet."

Yeats's resolve to seek a "singing school" and to study the models left by other artists may be seen as a resolve to forge another poetic style, one that could allow him to transform the events of his life into impersonal symbols in which others might recognize themselves. This does not mean abandoning the body but liberating the soul within the present body. On this side of eternity no soul exists without a body; the soul's desires will have to be fulfilled within the man's capacities to clap his hands and sing. Mentally the poet has set sail away from the self-imposed limitations of envy, toward a new exercise of his sense of possibility.

The Golden Detachment of Art

Once Yeats has averted his obsessive gaze from the sexual pairs that occupy center stage at the opening of the poem, he is able, in stanza III, to see other human figures with whom he can identify: sages, or singing-masters—figures that have been waiting in the periphery (a common occurrence when a significant change of perspective increases our awareness of others, as for example when a newly pregnant woman notices with astonishment the number of pregnant women she suddenly sees around her). For Yeats, these are wisdom-figures like those depicted in the mosaics of Byzantine churches: "sages standing in God's holy fire / As in the gold mosaic of a wall."

In a note accompanying "Sailing to Byzantium" in his *Collected Poems,* Yeats explains the specific reference to Byzantium:

> I think that if I could be given a month of antiquity and leave to spend it where I chose, I would spend it in Byzantium a little before Justinian opened St. Sophia and closed the Academy of Plato. . . . I think that in early Byzantium, maybe never before or since in recorded history, religious, aesthetic, and practical life were one, that architects and artificers . . . spoke to the multitude in gold and silver. The painter, the mosaic worker, the worker in gold and silver, the illuminator of sacred books were almost impersonal, almost perhaps without the consciousness of individual design, absorbed in their subject matter and that the vision of a whole people.

The meaning of these sages can be understood without Yeats's scholarly gloss, however, if we call to mind examples of Byzantine stylization. Each figure in a Byzantine mosaic stands rigidly erect, with drapery falling in folds like the inflexible fluting on a stone column, obscuring all physical characteristics of the body it covers. The faces, in contrast, express a lively though solemn intensity; the pupils of the eyes seem always to be fixed on the beholder with commanding intent. These sages, purged of envy, lust, greed, and other afflictions that spring from narrow egotism, express the power of vital spirituality in a fully human form. And what we find expressed in their imagery is a spirituality more intense for its being anonymous. Yeats's prayer to the sages, "Come from the holy fire . . . / And be the singing-masters of my soul," is thus for mastery of just such an impersonal style that will express the enduring insights of the soul, not the ego-bound illusion of a desire that cannot be fulfilled.

Most interpretations of "Sailing to Byzantium" assume that the transcendence Yeats seeks is expressed in the last stanza, in which he envisions being "out of nature" at last, and swears,

> I shall never take
> My bodily form from any natural thing,
> But such a form as Grecian goldsmiths make
> Of hammered gold and gold enameling.

But I find "Sailing to Byzantium" a poem that seeks fulfillment of desire *within*, not beyond, the limitations imposed by the real world. The golden "form" of stanza IV is a symbol for poetry itself. More specifically it is a symbol for an impersonal poetry, not expressive of an ephemeral mood or a particular situation. A poetry purged of the merely personal has the power to transcend its occasion, hence to sing tirelessly down through the generations about human themes that never change: the insufficiency of physical pleasure to satisfy the longing of our souls, the power of art to transform and elevate our visions of the possible, the brevity and preciousness of "whatever is begotten, born, and dies."

The golden bird symbolizes such poetry; it is a form expressive of *both* singing and artifice. Bird song is instinctual and nonreflective. Human song is the product of will and imagination. There is nothing analogous in the two modes of creation practiced by bird and poet. This is particularly true of the mode of creation practiced by Yeats. "Sailing to Byzantium," for example, went through twenty drafts before completion, totally changing theme and symbolism in the process. The poet's art is labor, like that of the goldsmith, who takes his material from mines in nature and transforms it through skill and effort into a medium of revelation, a form able "to sing / To lords and ladies . . . / Of what is past, or passing, or to come."

The last stanza of "Sailing to Byzantium" brings us full circle, back to a land of sensual music: to the ears of a drowsy emperor, to an assemblage of lords and ladies—sexual pairs. The realms of heart and artifice have been reunited. Having converted his envy and despair into insight, and having mastered a new form of song, the poet is able to return to stanza I's world of "dying generations" with golden detachment. The poem is the record of his self-liberation, a model of the creative process by which the sickness of the heart has been—and may in the future be—transformed. The process begins when our suffering has grown so acute we can no longer endure life in our present state; it can end in wisdom, when our need has made us seek those "monuments of unaging intellect" that speak to us personally, allowing us to recognize suffering as a necessary aspect of our existence as beings that grow and change. Miraculously, this recognition can liberate the sufferer, bringing him or her back to life with new capacities for song.

Limits of Willpower: Louise Bogan's "The Alchemist"

At the end of "Sailing to Byzantium," it is a work of art, not a human being, that sings serenely from its tree of knowledge "of what is past, or passing, or to come." No living creature is either pure or changeless. Yet the desire to change and the effort to change are often motivated by the illusion that, by willing it, we may totally transform ourselves. This illusion is the subject of Louise Bogan's fine lyric:

The Alchemist

I burned my life, that I might find
A passion wholly of the mind,
Thought divorced from eye and bone,
Ecstasy come to breath alone.
I broke my life, to seek relief
From the flawed light of love and grief.

With mounting beat the utter fire
Charred existence and desire.
It died low, ceased its sudden thresh.
I had found unmysterious flesh—
Not the mind's avid substance—still
Passionate beyond the will.

Exceptional in its own right, "The Alchemist," written when Louise Bogan was about twenty-five, grows even more interesting when read in the context of "Sailing to Byzantium." "The Alchemist" concerns the struggle to transcend fleshly desire in order to achieve spiritual ecstasy. This longing for transcendence arrives in the poem directly out of the philosophical tradition that originated with Plato, who divided existence into two realms: matter and spirit. Only through extreme moral and physical discipline could the human spirit, enmeshed in matter, purge and clarify itself during earthly life. In Plato's writings Socrates remains a figure solidly physical: eating, chatting, even sleeping in the course of pursuing wisdom. But later Platonists increasingly emphasized denial of appetite and exalted habits of asceticism. Hence Porphyry, biographer of Plotinus, the most influential of the Neoplatonist philosophers, says that Plotinus seemed ashamed of needing a body. "So deeply rooted was this feeling," Porphyry writes, "that he never could be induced to tell of his ancestry, his parentage, or his birthplace." When he was urged to allow a portrait to be made of himself, "he showed an unconquerable reluctance," asking, " 'Is it not enough to carry about this image in which nature has enclosed us?' "

Louise Bogan was neither a philosopher nor an ascetic. But she maintained a strict distinction between the narrator in her poems and the real woman who wrote them. From her point of view facts about an artist's life usually intruded upon the project of his or her art. As a consequence, aside from matters of public record, such as dates of publications and dates of birth and death (1897-1970), little biographical information is available that sheds light on her poetry. For fifty years she made her living as a writer of poems, stories, articles, translations, and book reviews for such periodicals as *The New Republic, The Nation,* and *The New Yorker.* But throughout her lifetime she avoided being interviewed or discussing her private affairs for public consumption.

Since her death, publication of a selection of her letters indicates that she could be wittily self-revealing among friends, but one letter—written, but never mailed, in response to a questionnaire—expresses pungently her aversion to talking about herself to strangers: "My dislike of telling future research students anything about myself is intense and profound. I believe the less authentic records are, the more 'interesting' they automatically become."

Considering the explicit and passionate nature of poems such as "The Alchemist," the extreme care Louise Bogan took to avoid giving out mere information is itself significant. A ruthless self-critic, Bogan wanted to maintain tight contol of the "I" she presented, in print, to the world. Even her briefest book reviews were written with a severe concern for style: "I *cut* and *cut* my sentences, right up to the last version; always keeping the adjectives down to a minimum and the adverbs practically down to zero." She was even more strict about her poetry. Though she wrote for over forty years, her definitive collection, *The Blue Estuaries: Poems 1923-1968,* contains only 105 poems. Many poets decide not to republish earlier poems when they make collections of their work. But Bogan appears to have seized these occasions as opportunities to scrutinize and discard old identities. One letter to an editor conveys this impulse to self-censorship. Recommending that a poem from a previous book be dropped, she explains, "It isn't that I'm turning on my early self. But the girl of 23 and 24, who wrote most of these early poems, was so seldom mawkish, that I want her not to be mawkish at all."

"The Alchemist" is one poem that survived every sweep of Bogan's scythe. Not at all mawkish, it displays her characteristic strengths. Like Yeats, Bogan usually preferred to write in rhymed stanzas—a very artificial arrangement of words—but to keep to the syntax of simple, declarative statements made in normal conversation: "I broke my life, to seek relief"; "I had found unmysterious flesh." This strategy of making a direct statement in the past tense gives a pronounced tone of authority to "The Alchemist." The tone of authority is much enhanced by the presence of strongly marked rhythm and exact rhyme. Every syllable of the poem is under firm control.

Yet, from the standpoint of theme, "The Alchemist" expresses a profound skepticism regarding the very *will* to control things. The poem is, paradoxically, at once an expression of mastery and a critique of the master, a paradox achieved through Bogan's decision to make the speaker of these words not a poet but an alchemist.

The Alchemist as Symbol

Alchemy developed from one of the earliest human efforts to create an exact science that would combine philosophy and technology. The first alchemists were Alexandrian metalworkers who, like Yeats's Grecian goldsmith, made precious objects "of hammered gold and gold enameling," as well as objects of less precious metals. Under the influence of Greek philosophy, and later of astrology, alchemists believed that they might discover the principles and devise the methods by which baser metals could be transmuted into pure gold. To protect their secrets, they often attempted to conceal the chemical processes and agents they used under symbolic names, usually derived from astrology. Eventually, alchemical treatises with their esoteric symbolisms were absorbed into other mystical philosophies, also influenced by astrology, that concerned the perfecting of the soul. For the alchemist, gold was not only the most valuable metal but also the most spiritual.

As a consequence of these origins, the alchemist is a complex figure in social history. He comes down to us either as a man of vast esoteric learning or a con man, and sometimes both. As a man who had attained enormous learning and thereby seemed to have acquired almost magical control over nature, the alchemist can be viewed as a precursor of the early atomic scientist of our own century during the pretechnological phase in the development of modern physics—the period when Louise Bogan wrote this poem. ("The Alchemist" was published in 1926, "Sailing to Byzantium" in 1927.) Men like Max Planck, Niels Bohr, and Albert Einstein attained the status of heroes in the popular imagination because they manifested, it seemed, the power of pure intellect to disclose secrets held in time, space, and matter.

Both facets of the alchemist as a historical figure—his noble dedication to knowledge and the deluded premises of his research—are active in Bogan's poem. "The Alchemist," however, is not a poem about alchemy per se. It is about the desire to attain a pure state of being, by purging the self of its contaminants. The metaphorical gold the alchemist seeks is named carefully in four qualified nouns: "*passion* wholly of the mind"; "*thought* divorced from eye and bone"; "*ecstasy* come to breath alone"; "the mind's avid *substance*" (italics added). The speaker in "The Alchemist" is driven to this radical and self-destructive effort ("I burned my life"; "I broke my life") by the torment of undergoing "love and grief"—the consequences of being impure, or human. Like the aged man in "Sailing to Byzantium," the alchemist is a being "sick with desire."

In an effort to attain a state of "pure" imagination, poets and other idealists throughout history have tried many experiments on themselves. Through the alchemy of drugs or forms of occult research they have sought to bring about in themselves a transmutation of consciousness, Bogan's "passion wholly of the mind." However, "The Alchemist" is a poem written in rejection of the theory that the highest art is the product of an abnormal consciousness, for the alchemist's experiment is an instructive failure. Seeking a pure passion, the alchemist does indeed find in the crucible something in a pure form, but it is not the form of thought, "the mind's avid substance." It is the form of "unmysterious flesh / . . . still / Passionate, beyond the will." Elizabeth Hardwick's remark, "the body is a poor vessel for transcendence," is countered in this poem: Bogan insists that it is the only vessel available. "The Alchemist" ends with a powerful affirmation of sensuous existence— the pure energy of life itself, ever changing and stubbornly diverse, willing its own survival.

Unmysterious Flesh

At yet another level, the one most interesting to me, "The Alchemist" is a very personal poem with meanings that emerge when viewed in the context of other poems by Louise Bogan. It is at the personal level that the will to deny the body, expressed in "The Alchemist," grows poignantly comprehensible. Such an interpretation of the poem begins with the question, who is the speaker? Not, apparently, a woman.

In the history of alchemy there are very few women. Intellectual power, spiritual authority, the commitment to solitude and self-discipline necessary to the alchemist—and to the poet—in Western culture have been regarded as "masculine" attainments. From the beginning of her career, Bogan's poetry reflects an uneasy acceptance of the idea that aspiration to intellectual power is a contradiction of the "feminine." This contradiction is rarely expressed in direct statement; rather, it infuses most of the poems that, like "The Alchemist," deal with a conflict between mental power and sexual passion. Throughout Bogan's work, this conflict is expressed in metaphors where "flesh" and "breath" form fateful polarities. "Flesh" is mortal, dumb, blind, helplessly instinctual; it is low, associated with darkness and the earth, and it is feminine. "Breath," by contrast, is the medium of inspiration, speech, music—high achievements, not associated with the feminine sphere. This polarity is the explicit theme of a powerful poem, "Cassandra," in which Bogan imagines Cassandra's clairvoyance as a consequence of liberation from feminine roles:

Cassandra

> To me, one silly task is like another.
> I bare the shambling tricks of lust and pride.
> This flesh will never give a child its mother,—
> Song, like a wing, tears through my breast, my side,
> And madness chooses out my voice again,
> Again. I am the chosen no hand saves:
> The shrieking heaven lifted over men,
> Not the dumb earth, wherein they set their graves.

Cassandra was a priestess whose accurate prophecies were ignored by the princes of Troy, a punishment Apollo ordained when she withheld promised sexual favors. She paid a high price for her ascent from femininity. In this respect, "Cassandra" is typical, for in Bogan's vision woman is frighteningly bound to and by her sexuality. It brings her low. In "The Crows," for example, Bogan likens an old woman who is still full of sexual passion to a harvested field, in which "there is only bitter / Winter-burning." The girl in "Chanson un Peu Naïve" is a "body... ploughed, / Sown, and broken yearly." Another, in "Girl's Song," lies with her lover in a field as on a grave: "And, since she loves [him], and she must, / Puts her young cheek against the dust."

In these lyrics, Bogan is working with stereotypes of the feminine from which she, as author, maintains a knowing distance. These are *some* women, *other* women. Yet the same conflicting opposites—low/ high, flesh/breath, feminine/masculine—furnish the imagery in which Bogan speaks as "I" describing her own creative powers. In these poems, as in "The Alchemist," the speaker seeks to purify herself of personal history, to become "thought divorced from eye and bone."

In attempting to "rise above" her femininity and become a poet, however, Bogan does not seek to transform herself into a man. She seeks to be an imagination freed of body, or, in the imagery of "The Alchemist," she seeks to turn a base metal into gold. The base metal is her female body, the material prison of "the mind's avid substance." Just as gold was thought by alchemists to be the essential metal resident within all others, accessible through a rearrangement of molecules, so Bogan the alchemist assumes that a body-denying passion wholly of the mind must be the highest state attainable. Fortunately, she survives this self-inflicted attack; the residue in the crucible is her own humanity. Hence, failure of the alchemist in her can be seen as a liberation of the whole person. The poem ends on a note of self-mocking relief, wry rather than bitter: "I found unmysterious flesh." With this line she accepts herself in all her complexity; implicitly, she accepts her sex.

Like Yeats's "Sailing to Byzantium," then, Bogan's "The Alchemist" concerns a new synthesis of the actual with the ideal. In both poems the narrators are liberated from false objects of desire by the keenness of their need for an ideal that can withstand scrutiny from the perspective of reality. Both poems, finally, affirm the truthfulness of the imagination, insisting on reality as the basis of its flight. For the greatest art flings its imagery into a zone still controlled by gravity, where freedom tests itself against necessity: the hawk floating in a measurable updraft, its beauty sensed as a momentary mastery of incessantly contending forces.

CHAPTER FOUR

Three Mirrors Reflecting Women: Poetry of Sylvia Plath, Anne Sexton, and Adrienne Rich

IN 1905 MARY CASSATT painted a large canvas that shows, in brilliant yellows and soft greens, a seated woman with a nude little blonde girl in her lap. Pinned to the woman's dress is a large sunflower. Behind them on the wall is a mirror, reflecting the pair in profile. A second mirror, held up in both hands by the child with the woman's help, reflects the child's face.

Cassatt (1844-1926) is often described as America's greatest woman painter. She spent her working life in Paris among the Impressionists and became a good friend of Degas, who helped promote her work. Her mature style, however, is distinctively her own, recognizable chiefly in her experimental handling of the figures of women and children. The subject itself enhanced her popularity in the prewar era, dominated still by the Victorian idealization of the family, but Cassatt's treatment of these figures, while intimate, never suggests anecdote or allegory. In fact, she rarely gave her paintings titles. Much like the human figures in Toulouse-Lautrec's café interiors, Cassatt's subjects seem less chosen than found. However arresting the configurations they present, they seem to have arrived in the painting merely as familiar objects commonplace in the painter's surroundings. In her canvases women, reflected in mirrors, braid their hair or try on dresses for seamstresses. Children are bathed, nursed, set out to play in gardens. That the painter was a woman gave her, perhaps, privileged access to these protected worlds. That the woman was a painter made these worlds accessible to art.

In the past decade, Mary Cassatt's work has attracted new attention, stimulated in part by the women's movement. Because she was a painter respected in her own right by influential peers, discussing Cassatt's work has become a way of discussing other more general questions in aesthetics: what does it mean to designate an artist a *woman* painter, a *woman* sculptor, a *woman* poet? Does consciousness itself have sexual characteristics? Is there such a thing as a feminine vision or a feminine style? The pair of mirrors in Mary Cassatt's untitled painting, which offer a double perspective on two female figures, makes a point of departure for discussing three contemporary poets whose work poses some of these same questions.

Throughout the preceding chapters I have been discussing life themes in modern poetry as if it were possible to do so without reference to race, class, and sex—to speak of the life of Man, as if experience had a universal dimension. However, since World War II, a number of important poets have emerged who have written new forms of poetry in which considerations of race, class, and sex are inseparable from the meanings of the poems—indeed, are often their subjects. These poets have enlarged the dimensions of literature, making it able to say things unheard before. Some of them are women.

The appearance of women in the history of poetry, as in the history of painting, has until recently been the manifestation of a social contradiction. Poetry, like other intellectual and spiritual disciplines, has been a male province. Women wrote poetry, of course, but to the female writer a special name was given—*poetess,* which did not mean *poet.* The poet held a special position of authority in culture. In England that authority was socially acknowledged in the eighteenth-century creation of the public office of poet laureate, appointed by the king. In America, struggling to define authority in non-European terms, Walt Whitman in the preface to the first edition of his *Leaves of Grass* described the poet's function as that of referee:

> Of all nations the United States with veins full of poetical stuff most need poets and will doubtless have the greatest and use them the greatest. Their Presidents shall not be their common referee so much as their poets shall. Of all mankind the great poet is the equable man. . . . He bestows on every object or quality its fit proportions neither more nor less. He is the

> arbiter of the diverse and he is the key. . . . Obedience does not master him, he masters it. High up out of reach he stands turning a concentrated light. . . . he is judgment. He judges not as the judge judges but as the sun falling around a helpless thing.

Latent in this lyric description of the poet are two assumptions. First, that the poet is a sort of spiritual chief of state and, like other figures of authority in the state, thoroughly patriarchal in the investitures of his power; presidents, arbiters, judges—all men "high up out of reach"—are his peers. Second, the poet's intelligence is like the light of the sun, that is, it sheds not a special perspective but a universal truth. The poet is thus the transmitter, rather than the originator, of the knowledge his poem expresses.

The image of the poet as the masculine chief of state in charge of dispensing universal spiritual truths persists influentially into the modern period until after World War II. The dominant voices in English poetry before World War II were those of Yeats, Pound, and Eliot, each of whom undertook to write an inclusive history of man, unified by a perception of continuity or tradition: Yeats in *A Vision,* Pound in *Cantos,* Eliot in *The Waste Land* and *Four Quartets.* Eliot spoke for all three in his essay "Tradition and the Individual Talent":

> Tradition . . . cannot be inherited, and if you want it you must obtain it by great labor. It involves, in the first place, the historical sense, which we may call nearly indispensable to any one who would continue to be a poet beyond his twenty-fifth year; and the historical sense involves a perception, not only of the pastness of the past, but of its presence; the historical sense compels a man to write not merely with his own generation in his bones, but with a feeling that the whole of the literature of Europe from Homer and within it the whole of the literature of his own country has a simultaneous existence and composes a simultaneous order. . . . No poet, no artist of any art, has his complete meaning alone. His significance, his appreciation is the appreciation of his relation to the dead poets and artists.

Contemporary poetry—poetry written since 1945—has largely abandoned the idea that there are universal truths and, with it, the quest for continuity and its corollary emphasis on the Great Man. Since 1945 a number of new poets have gained recognition, among whom the names of Sylvia Plath, Anne Sexton, and Adrienne Rich are as prominent as the names Robert Lowell, Allen Ginsberg, and Gary Snyder. Spiritual authority no longer seems the exclusive province of men, and women writers seem less confined to certain types of subject matter by the expectations of their audiences. The term "poetess" is now seldom used. Rather, women have extended the expressive capacities of poetry itself by adding to it their own subjectivities. As in Mary Cassatt's painting, mirrors have appeared authoritatively in the hands of women, and what they reflect are female lives viewed from different angles. I would like to look into a number of the mirrors held up in the poems of these women.

First Mirror: Mother and Child—Sylvia Plath's "Morning Song"

Sylvia Plath is one of several contemporary writers often referred to as confessional poets. Theodore Roethke, Robert Lowell, John Berryman, Allen Ginsberg, and Anne Sexton are others associated with this genre. Different as they are, they write in frankly autobiographical terms about subject matter previously regarded as innappropriate in art. Family quarrels, alcoholism, mental institutions, complicated sexuality, various forms of social humiliation—all are explored from a personal perspective in this poetry.

The term *confessional* is misleading, however, to the degree that it suggests that the poet writes poems to unburden his or her conscience. Confession is an act of admitting guilt or disclosing other things formerly known to oneself but hidden from others out of shame. Confessional poetry, however, is an act of creation, performed not for the poet's sake alone (in the sense that confession is good for the soul) but for the sake of art itself: to make poetry more inclusive. Confessional poetry reaches into areas of experience formerly considered compromising to the poet's authority. When T.S. Eliot, for example, writes in *The Waste Land* of sexual torment, he displaces onto the mythical figures of the Fisher King and Tiresias what biographical information indicates was his own horror:

> And I Tiresias have foresuffered all
> Enacted on this same divan or bed;
> I who have sat by Thebes below the wall
> And walked among the lowest of the dead.

To achieve the authority of spokesman for the universal dimensions of personal pain, Eliot avoids representing it as personal. But Sylvia Plath and other contemporary poets anchor the universal in the structure of first-person narrative. The world of each of Plath's poems is not timeless; it is a finite, temporal, and subjective world. Yet it is important to see that both mythic allusions and personal references in poetry are equally poetic, that is, equally made up. Thus, when asked in an interview whether she believed her poetry was confession, Anne Sexton responded, "I've got to say it's not exactly... because I'll often confess to things that never happened.... If I did all the things I confess to, there would be no time to write a poem. ... I'll often assume the first person and tell someone else's story." Describing the origins of her own poems, Sylvia Plath emphasized the role of control in the process of converting experience into poetry:

> I think my poems come immediately out of the sensuous and emotional experiences I have, but I must say I cannot sympa-thize with these cries from the heart that are informed by nothing except a needle or a knife or whatever it is. I believe that one should be able to control and manipulate experiences, even the most terrifying—like madness, being tortured, this kind of experience—and one should be able to manipulate these experiences with an informed and intelligent mind. I think that personal experience shouldn't be a kind of shut box and mirror-looking narcissistic experience. I believe it should be generally relevant, to such things as Hiroshima and Dachau, and so on [from *The Art of Sylvia Plath*].

Liberation From Cliché

The confessional poem, then, is like a lens that magnifies and orga-nizes particulars, a mirror that for an instant frames an identity. And very often the subject of the confessional poem is the need for such clarification, and the related discovery that old definitions are useless in helping one to recognize oneself in a traumatic context. Some terms describing feminine roles—such as "maiden," "spinster," "mistress"— have become anachronistic. Even the term "woman" contains a kind of ambiguity. Whereas "female" denotes biological identity, "woman" denotes a social role that varies from culture to culture. This ambiguity becomes a space for creation.

In Mary Cassatt's paintings of women with children, for example, the refusal to sentimentalize the subject is an aspect of meaning. In some of Mary Cassatt's most interesting canvases the human figures have been neutralized to the status of objects, elements of design. The dressed-up woman holding the nude child in the painting described earlier is a good example. The child's flesh tones and blond hair complement the woman's finery; no other relation can be established with certainty between them, except those provided by the mirrors. One feels the absence of conventional symbolism as a statement in its own right: the artist has liberated this pair of figures from cliché. A similar rejection of convention is visible in many of Sylvia Plath's finest poems, including one entitled "Morning Song," in which her subject, like Cassatt's, is a woman looking at a child:

Morning Song

Love set you going like a fat gold watch.
The midwife slapped your footsoles, and your bald cry
Took its place among the elements.

Our voices echo, magnifying your arrival. New statue.
In a drafty museum, your nakedness
Shadows our safety. We stand round blankly as walls.

I'm no more your mother
Than the cloud that distils a mirror to reflect its own slow
Effacement at the wind's hand.

All night your moth-breath
Flickers among the flat pink roses. I wake to listen:
A far sea moves in my ear.

One cry, and I stumble from bed, cow-heavy and floral
In my Victorian nightgown.
Your mouth opens clean as a cat's. The window square

Whitens and swallows its dull stars. And now you try
Your handful of notes;
The clear vowels rise like balloons.

The feeling in this poem is a mother's uneasy sense of the unrecognizability of her newborn infant—a feeling quite different from those we normally call "maternal." Plath identifies the qualities of this feeling in a complicated metaphor:

I'm no more your mother
Than the cloud that distils a mirror to reflect its own slow
Effacement at the wind's hand.

A superficial reading suggests that these lines say, I'm no more your mother than the cloud is your mother. But the particulars of the image convey more. The terms of identification could be schematized thus: *I* is to *mother* as *cloud* is to *mirror that reflects the cloud's own slow efface-ment*. The concept of mother and clouded mirror are brought together to convey the woman's fear that she may disappear under the influence of the child's wearing demands. To mother an infant is to dedicate one's energy to its survival; the poem emphasizes the oppressive imperious-ness of the child's need: "I wake to listen"; "I stumble from bed, cow-heavy." The term *I* brought together with *cloud* conveys the newly delivered woman's sense of being suddenly formless, indefinite until bounded by a mirror such as the term "mother." But the cloud distills its image in a mirror only to find itself in a process of effacement. The *I* rejects this distillation into *mother*. The poem is an effort to reflect more accurately her relationship to the child.

That relationship is the subject of the other stanzas. There Plath emphasizes the child's total otherness, conveyed from the poem's first lines in images of sound. The child first announces itself as a heartbeat: "love set you going like a fat gold watch," an audible otherness within the mother; it comes into the world as a "bald cry," haunting the mother's consciousness with its light breath, demanding her breast with its morning song. "You," she calls the child merely, seeking to convey its separateness from herself, its disturbing and touching newness—avoiding any descriptive terms that would fit the child into any social category, including that of sex. Her descriptive metaphors do not even humanize the child: "new statue" she calls it; "your moth-breath / Flickers among the flat pink roses. . . . / Your mouth opens clean as a cat's."

The early hour and the atmosphere of postnatal exhaustion enhance the woman's dreamlike sense of strangeness and dissociation from the child. Plath is exploring that early moment of maternity before the identity "mother" has settled into the woman's consciousness—before the relationship mother-child has been established. Just as adults bestow identity on babies by giving them family names and nicknames, new-born infants bestow motherhood on women. Psychologists tell us a sense of individual identity begins to develop in infancy partly through eye contact. Plath is observing the same thing about the bestowal of identity on a mother. This infant and mother are still connected by the primal bond of flesh: the woman's breast growing cow-heavy in response to the child's cry—the unlearned response of the woman's endocrine system. But the bond of human recognition is undeveloped in either of them at the moment treated in the poem. It is a time, for the woman, fraught with uneasiness: "your nakedness / Shadows our safety. We stand round blankly as walls." Yet the feelings in this poem are, I think, those of the deepest human love: love that recognizes the complete uniqueness of its object. This feeling permeates the poem and is visible in the woman's avoidance of labeling the baby "mine." It is conveyed as well in the tender description of the baby's crying in the last lines: "you try / Your handful of notes; / The clear vowels rise like balloons." The noises that call the mother to the baby's side are perceived as pieces of syllables, potential forms of communication. As the poem's last image they are tentatively affectionate and festive, a handful of possible meanings gathering in the air above the pair with a shadowy gaiety.

Could Plath's "Morning Song" have been written by a man? This question inevitably arises in any discussion of the relevance to art of the sexual basis of consciousness. No mind walks around free of a body; every hand writing a poem is connected to a nervous system stoked with experiences engendered by sexual identity. In "Morning Song," for example, the tug of milk in the breasts that makes the mother cow-heavy is an experience unique to lactating women. On the other hand, the identity-obliterating sense of change described in "Morning Song" is common to both parents, especially with the birth of a first child. Remembering the way Tolstoy portrays childbirth in *Anna Karenina,* it is possible to imagine as the author of "Morning Song" a man exceptionally observant of women and sensitive to their inner lives. Empathy is a writer's most important emotional resource.

The Confessional Poem as an Act of Disclosure

Still, "Morning Song" represents something new in poetry. Twenty-five years earlier this subject probably would not have appeared in poetry, which was reserved for higher things. Partly because of Plath's example, the experience of women has become in poetry a subject with an authority of its own. But postwar poetry in general is more subjective than the poetry of earlier periods. The genre of confessional poetry seems to have developed for the very purpose of admitting the realm of subjectivity more fully into art. For confessional poetry, as "Morning Song" illustrates, is not the same thing as autobiography, in which the writer's purpose is usually to describe exemplary experience—a significant education, a life-crisis successfully resolved. The confessional poem is not a model of successful emotional management; it is an act of disclosure, in which experience is always richer than any ideas about it expressed in examples, conventions, or stereotypes.

I have lingered over the distinction between confession and confessional poetry because it is necessary to keep it in mind in order to see Sylvia Plath as a poet at all. Her death by suicide at the age of thirty-one is such a well-known fact that her art is almost inevitably discussed in its grim light. Consequently, much of the popular interest in Plath has a morbid quality; fascinated by her death, readers come to her poems looking for evidence of fatal sickness.

Yet when one turns to a poem by Sylvia Plath, one finds, whatever the subject, a ravishing lucidity. Her suicide should not be permitted to contaminate our perception of the accuracy of her vision or what she accomplished with it in her art. As she affirmed in the passage I quoted earlier, "One should be able to control and manipulate experience, even the most terrifying—like madness, being tortured, . . . and one should be able to manipulate these experiences with an informed and intelligent mind."

Plath's art supports the thesis of Hannah Arendt in *The Life of the Mind*. Taking her example from Adolf Eichmann's trial in Jerusalem, Arendt observes that evil in the modern world frequently expresses itself in a rigor of mindlessness: "Clichés, stock phrases, adherence to conventional, standardized codes of expression and conduct have the socially recognized function of protecting us against reality, that is, against the claim on our thinking attention that all events and facts make by virtue of their existence. If we were responsive to this claim all the time we would soon be exhausted; Eichmann differed from the rest of us only in that he clearly knew of no such claim at all. . . . Is wickedness, however we may define it . . . *not* a necessary condition for evil-doing? Might the problem of good and evil, our faculty for telling right from wrong, be connected with our faculty of thought?"

Plath contributed to modern art, in a handful of poems, a handful of mirrors each of which said, "If you think you recognize this person, look again." For Plath was agonized over the power of convention in our lives, the mindlessness with which we label things in the world, thus prolonging our illusion that we know them. Confessional poetry as a genre attacks the very gesture of generalization, the fiction of objectivity. All thought, all comprehension, originates in a subjectivity with its own drives toward knowledge. Confessional poetry embeds that truth in its very form. As in "Morning Song," it gives us a mind distilling itself for a moment in the frame of our attention.

Second Mirror: Fairy Tale Virgin—Anne Sexton's "The Frog Prince"

The bedtime story is one of the rituals of child-raising. It provides a privileged moment between parents and children, drawing them close together for a while in another world. One of the chief pleasures for adults in this ritual is the sense of sharing: parents enjoy reading aloud stories they liked themselves as children. Consequently certain children's books become classics, handed down from generation to generation. Within the field of children's literature, fairy tales have shown a special power of survival. The cold-blooded violence and magical unreality of their content has caused them occasionally to fall out of favor with teachers, librarians, and parents. But children for hundreds of years, right up to the present, have responded to them with profound fascination. Child psychologist Bruno Bettelheim theorizes in *The Uses of Enchantment* that this is because children are exposed to fairy tales at a crucial period of development when, in order to relinquish infantile dependency, they are coming to terms with many forms of anxiety. The fairy tale, according to Bettelheim, addresses those anxieties directly and builds them into imaginative structures that sort out good from bad, helping a child develop a sense of how to master hardships. Fairy tales offer an effective form of moral instruction; yet their path to the mind is delight.

The perception that fairy tales carry significant messages under the sugar coating of their magic plots lies behind the book *Transformations* by Anne Sexton. Her curiosity piqued by her seventeen-year-old daughter's continual rereading of a book of Grimm's fairy tales, Sexton began to study them herself. What emerged was one of Sexton's strongest books: witty versions in poetry of seventeen tales. These were such a departure from her previous highly successful poetry in the confessional mode that her publishers were reluctant to print them. "I realize that the 'Transformations' . . . lack the intensity and perhaps some of the confessional force of my previous work," she wrote to her editor, "[but] they are just as much about me as my other poetry."

Anne Sexton became, by saying much about herself, a very popular poet in her lifetime. She began writing professionally at the age of twenty-nine during one of the bouts of mental illness that corroded her life. In eighteen years of writing she published nine books of poetry, one of which won a Pulitzer Prize. Her life ended in suicide in 1974. Sexton's death, like Sylvia Plath's, is such a compelling biographical fact that it is tempting to view her poetry as a window into human self-destruction. However, Sexton's letters indicate that she viewed her poems as the products of her health. Prey to violent, rapid mood swings, Sexton distinguished in herself a "good Anne" and a "bad Anne." The good Anne, the poet, was the one capable of self-transcending communication. "I am given to excess," she wrote to a friend; "I have found that I can control it best in a poem . . . if the poem is good then it will have the excess under control . . . it is the core of the poem . . . there like stunted fruit, unseen but actual [Sexton's punctuation]."

Fairy Tales for Adults

The fairy tales that caught Sexton's imaginative eye were mainly those ending "and they lived happily ever after"—stories in which a beautiful maiden is won by a clever man. As Bettelheim observes, most stories of this type leave us in the dark about the heroine's feelings. She—or rather her beauty, which symbolizes her suitability as an object of desire—is merely the cause of the hero's struggles and his reward for success. Sexton's poems query that symbol of maidenly complacency much as Plath in "Morning Song" queries the conventional image of mother and child. Without changing the contours of fairy tale plots, Sexton transforms them into stories addressed to the imaginations of adults, who at certain stages also need assistance in achieving inner growth.

In Sexton's versions, however, the element of moral instruction is overt: her stories deal in one way or another with the heroine's relation to her sexuality. In retelling "Snow White and the Seven Dwarfs," for example, Sexton identifies the old queen's vanity and the virginal emptiness of Snow White as two phases of the same mindlessness, a consequence of the narcissism augmented in women throughout life by the admiration of Prince Charming. Her "Snow White" ends not with a dissolve into "happily ever after" but with a disturbingly futuristic image:

> Meanwhile Snow White held court,
> rolling her china-blue doll eyes open and shut
> and sometimes referring to her mirror
> as women do.

"Rapunzel" becomes, under Sexton's scrutiny, a story about the pathos of an older woman's sexual love for a younger woman until the latter grows up and can no longer be kept away from men. But the story that deals most explicitly with a woman's transformation through acceptance of her sexuality is Sexton's version of "The Frog Prince."

In Grimm's fairy tale of "The Frog Prince" a little princess while playing one day accidentally drops her golden ball into a well. A frog appears and, finding the princess distraught, says he will fetch the ball if she will promise to let him come home with her and eat from her plate, drink from her cup, and sleep in her bed. She promises, thinking contemptuously that no mere frog has a right to such intimacy. When the frog returns the ball she runs away with it. The next evening while she is eating dinner with her father, the frog comes to the door and reminds her of her promises. Her angry father, the king, forces her to fulfill them.

After much prodding she allows the frog to eat from her plate and drink from her cup. But when they are alone in her bedroom she becomes so disgusted by the frog that she hurls him against the wall. Instantly he turns into a handsome prince. They fall in love at once, marry, and go off to his homeland to reveal the change to his loved ones.

Two aspects of this tale receive special attention in Sexton's version: the symbolic meaning of the ball and the disguised identity of the frog. In Sexton's story, the plot gets under way with a question:

> Why
> should a certain
> quite adorable princess
> be walking in her garden
> at such a time
> and toss her golden ball
> up like a bubble
> and drop it into the well?
> It was ordained.
> Just as the fates deal out
> the plague with a tarot card.
> Just as the Supreme Being drills
> holes in our skulls to let
> the Boston Symphony through.
> . . . .
> Lost, she said,
> my moon, my butter calf,
> my yellow moth, my Hindu hare.
> Obviously it was more than a ball.
> Balls such as these are not
> for sale in Au Bon Marché.

The ball is the sexuality of the princess; its changing meaning reflects the transformation of the princess from child into woman. At first her ball is only a golden toy, something very nice with which to amuse herself. Then she loses it, through its dropping into someone else's territory: dark territory, inhabited by a creature she finds ugly and repulsive. Sexton's metaphors comparing the loss of the ball to getting the plague or suffering the "drill" of a Supreme Being both underscore the sexual significance of the event in the plot, and they convey adolescent hostility to the prospect of being an object of sexual desire. Still, this is the fate ordained for an adorable princess.

Once the ball is out of the princess's hands, she becomes involved in a fatal negotiation. She makes promises to the frog with childish ease, that is, without intending to keep them; but when the king steps in to enforce her commitments, the princess discovers she is in a situation governed by adult rules. She has been handed over by her father, the guardian of her sexuality.

This frog, fortunately, is really a prince; but the story is about the way the princess sees him. Why does the prince appear in the form of a frog? Bruno Bettelheim writes that "The Frog Prince," like "Beauty and the Beast," belongs to a subcategory of fairy tales termed the "animal groom cycle." Characteristically in this type of story it is the father who causes the maiden to accept the animal, which she does out of obedience, still behaving as a child. She does not really take responsibility for her actions until, alone with the frog, she is aggravated by disgust and abhorrence into a new sense of self, and asserts what and whom she will or will not love:

> She woke up aghast.
> I suffer for birds and fireflies
> but not frogs, she said,
> and threw him across the room.
> Kaboom!
>
> Like a genie coming out of a samovar,
> a handsome prince arose in the
> corner of her royal bedroom.
> He had kind eyes and hands
> and was a friend of sorrow.
> Thus they were married.
> After all he had compromised her.

The frog's transformation is startling and wholly unaccounted for in the poem. Further, as Bettelheim observes, it is characteristic of stories containing an animal groom that the reasons man was changed into animal remain unknown. This ambiguity in Grimm's fairy tale allows Sexton to draw her own conclusions about this frog who lives in a dark well, out of sight; who, though small and soft, frightens and disgusts the princess so much; who, finally, wants to be domesticated, taken indoors, and accepted into her daily life. In an early line of the poem Sexton reveals, "Frog is my father's genitals." This intuition about the frog's real identity permeates the realistic imagery with which the frog presents himself to the maiden in Sexton's version of the story:

> Suddenly the well grew
> thick and boiling
> and a frog appeared.
> His eyes bulged like two peas
> and his body was trussed into place.
> Do not be afraid, Princess,
> he said, I am not a vagabond,
> a cattle farmer, a shepherd,
> a doorkeeper, a postman
> or a laborer.
> I come to you as a tradesman.
> I have something to sell.
> Your ball, he said,
> for just three things.

With the frog's disappearance as frog, the metaphors describing the ball change too; the frame of reference is no longer the world of toys and animal pets, as when the ball is introduced:

> Lost, she said,
> my moon, my butter calf,
> my yellow moth, my Hindu hare.

Tenderly, the prince who has restored the ball to her takes care to see that no threat of loss can come to it:

> He hired a night watchman
> so that no one could enter the chamber
> and he had the well
> boarded over so that
> never again would she lose her ball,
> that moon, that Krishna hair,
> that blind poppy, that innocent globe.

Krishna is a god in Hindu mythology renowned as a lover. With the punning change from Hindu hare to Krishna hair, Sexton may be implying that the transformation from maiden to woman is as radical as the substitution of letters in a word that thereby changes its meaning without changing its sound. Or perhaps the reference to Krishna is there to remind us that his followers call on the divine name to transport them into ecstatic consciousness; the little girl's hare is now haré: haré Krishna, haré my erotic god. In any case, the closing lines of the poem are serene, tender, and unambivalent. The change from maiden to madonna—fruitful woman—is an accomplished emotional reality:

> never again would she lose her ball,
> that moon, that Krishna hair,
> that blind poppy, that innocent globe,
> that madonna womb.

Usurping the Silence of Unspoken Feelings

What Sexton has added to Grimm's tale is a point of view and a tone of voice. Fairy tales are famously without tone: the most blood-curdling events are narrated, like the most commonplace, in a perfectly matter-of-fact way. Sexton without in the least altering the plot of the fairy tale enriches its symbolism. She usurps the silence previously occupied by the heroine's unspoken feelings; she enters her consciousness and turns on the lights. The dynamic relationship thereby set up between Sexton's version and Grimm's may be compared to that created by the pair of mirrors in Mary Cassatt's painting. In Sexton's fairy tale, plot, like the background mirror, hangs in neutral territory, giving an impersonal account. The feminine point of view in Sexton's poem, like the hand mirror, lets us meet the gaze of a face we would otherwise view only in profile. Both mirrors are necessary to the composition, but the focal point of both painting and poem is that small mirror held up at a special angle by a woman's hand.

Third Mirror: The Survivor—Poems of Adrienne Rich

> Thinking of the sea I think of light
> lacing, lancing the water
> the blue knife of a radiant consciousness
> bent by the waves of vision as it pierces
> to the deepest grotto
>
> And I think of those lives we tried to live
> in our globed helmets, self-enclosed
> bodies self-illumined gliding
> safe from the turbulence
>
> and how, miraculously, we failed
>
> —from "The Wave"

In her book on motherhood, *Of Woman Born,* Adrienne Rich characterizes her situation in mid-life as a writer: "This book comes out of a double need to survive and work; and I wrote it in part for the young woman I once was, divided between body and mind, wanting to give her the book she was seeking." In her first five books of poems (up to 1970) Adrienne Rich wrote from the center of a contradiction that was slowly clarifying its terms in her consciousness: a contradiction between mind and body, between the work of a poet and the work of a mother and wife, between a man's world and woman's place. Her slow but thorough alienation from the social roles that shape the lives of women— white, contemporary, middle-class American women—accompanied a growing recognition of the ways women might draw support and intelligence from knowledge of each other's lives.

Dethroning Stereotypes

From 1970 on, Rich's art took a new direction. No longer were her poems merely acts of disclosure; they became—or were intended to become—instruments of change: "The words are purposes. / The words are maps," she wrote in "Diving into the Wreck"; "I wanted to choose words that even you / would have to be changed by," she wrote in "Implosions." In her writing Rich confronts particularly the stereotypes and clichés that dominate the lives of women in relation to men, trying to become that "light / lacing, lancing the water" of women's experience, that "blue knife of a radiant consciousness." To some extent this is the project also of the poems by Sylvia Plath and Anne Sexton that I discussed earlier. They seek to revitalize images of women as mothers and brides by enlivening them with intelligent feminine subjectivity. But Rich takes this work a giant step further. She seeks to dethrone stereotypes entirely by setting in their place images of women liberated from the isolation of family life. Where Plath and Sexton are revisionists, Rich becomes a mythmaker.

The nature of Rich's project cannot be understood from the example of one poem, for it is the product of an evolution that spans her thirty-year career as a poet and is still going on. Her story begins with "a young woman divided between body and mind" and takes her to the point where, at age forty-five, she is able to affirm in a love poem:

> Well, that's finished. The woman who cherished
> her suffering is dead. I am her descendant.
> I love the scar-tissue she handed on to me,
> but I want to go on from here with you
> fighting the temptation to make a career of pain.
>
> —from VIII, *Twenty-one Love Poems*

To Survive and Work

When Rich writes in *Of Woman Born,* "This book comes out of a double need to survive and work," she seems to be making a revision of Freud's often-quoted formula regarding human need. Asked as a therapist what he thought a normal person ought to be able to do well, Freud reportedly said, "Love and work." Rich substitutes "survive" for "love" in this double imperative, because from her point of view women need to learn modes of loving other than those they have traditionally learned from mothers, other adult women, and, especially, men. Rich observes that a woman dependent upon being *chosen* by a man in order to occupy a respected position in society is peculiarly susceptible to dreams of romantic love (the world-transforming magic of being chosen) and to sexual jealousy (the world-shattering fear of being abandoned). These twin themes in a woman's fantasy life have a common parent in narcissism, the idealization of self as an object of love—one consequence of the structure of patriarchal society, which conditions males to be the aggressors in sexual pairing.

Rich is suspicious of the word "love" when applied to women's desires for men. She treats this subject directly in "Translations":

Translations

> You show me the poems of some woman
> my age, or younger
> translated from your language

Certain words occur: *enemy, oven, sorrow*
enough to let me know
she's a woman of my time

obsessed

with Love, our subject:
we've trained it like ivy to our walls
baked it like bread in our ovens
worn it like lead on our ankles
watched it through binoculars as if
it were a helicopter
bringing food to our famine
or the satellite
of a hostile power

I begin to see that woman
doing things: stirring rice
ironing a skirt
typing a manuscript till dawn

trying to make a call
from a phonebooth

The phone rings unanswered
in a man's bedroom
she hears him telling someone else
Never mind. She'll get tired—
hears him telling her story to her sister

who becomes her enemy
and will in her own time
light her own way to sorrow

ignorant of the fact this way of grief
is shared, unnecessary
and political

1972

   Obsession with "Love, our subject" transcends social class, race,
and nationality, making women's lives recognizable to each other

through common experiences captured in certain key phrases with implications Rich calls political. A woman's anxious preoccupation with whether or not she is loved—loved enough, loved exclusively—is a waste of energy, irrational and insatiable. Worse, as Rich's military similes imply, this obsession alienates a woman not only from the man who rejects her but from the women who in her fantasies populate his bedroom. Alienated from other women, the woman obsessed with jealous love cannot know that this "way of grief"—her alternative to a way of life—is shared: the common lot of those conditioned to seek love in this way. Because sexual jealousy is a condition of suffering induced by a form of society in which people are regarded as possessions, such suffering can be regarded as both political and unnecessary—hence Rich's preference for *survival* rather than *love* as the subject on which to address the woman "divided between body and mind" and seeking wisdom on how to live. *Survive* is a more urgent directive than *love* as defined in women's lives in a time of cultural change. It implies an investment in life at a level more basic than that of family unit or social class.

By her own acknowledgement, Rich's personal sense of conflict between love and work came from the passion with which she had idealized and attempted to fulfill the traditional roles of mother and wife. In "When We Dead Awaken" she writes, "I plunged in my early twenties into marriage and had three children before I was thirty. . . . I had thought I was choosing a full life: the life available to most men, in which sexuality, work, and parenthood could coexist. But I felt, at 29, guilt toward the people closest to me, and guilty toward my own being." Yet it was the very depth of her commitment to both poles of the contradiction in her life—motherhood and poetry—that finally enabled Rich to achieve a creative revolution in perspective.

In terms that apply to Rich, Jean-Paul Sartre in *Between Existentialism and Marxism* meditates in old age on the processes by which contradictions in his own life had led to more and more radical stances politically, describing the ways a gifted intellectual brings his or her mind to bear on a problem that permeates existence so deeply it almost cannot be formulated: "It would be wrong to imagine that the intellectual could accomplish this task [of transcending the merely personal perspective on his struggles] by simply *studying* the ideology inculcated in him (for example by subjecting it to ordinary critical methods). In actual fact it is his *own* ideology—it manifests itself both in his mode of life . . . and in his Weltanschauung. In other words it is the tinted glasses through which he normally looks at the world. The contradiction from which he suffers is at first experienced only as suffering."

When Sartre speaks of suffering here, he does not refer to the obvious anguish of the lives of the poor, the racially oppressed, the social outcasts. He is speaking of those human beings whose affluence permits them leisure for contemplation, whose educations furnish them with tools of analysis and with historical and ethical perspectives, and whose integrity compels them to moral awareness—or what Hannah Arendt has described as the opposite of evil: mindfulness.

For women of Rich's generation, class, and abilities, mindfulness was a talent highly encouraged and cultivated—up to a point. Adrienne Rich, like Sylvia Plath, went through college winning the highest honors, including a fellowship year of postgraduate travel and study abroad. Then at an age when as a man she would have been ripe for graduate school or other professional training, she married. In "When We Dead Awaken" Rich recalls that women in the 1950s entered marriage with the same dedicated career-orientation that their men brought to professions:

> There was nothing overt in the environment to warn me: these were the fifties, and in reaction to the earlier wave of feminism, middle-class women were making careers of domestic perfection, working to send their husbands through professional schools, then retiring to raise large families. People were moving out to the suburbs, technology was going to be the answer to everything, even sex; the family was in its glory. Life was extremely private; women were isolated from each other by the loyalties of marriage. . . . I went on trying to write; my second book and first child appeared in the same month. But by the time that book came out I was already dissatisfied with those poems, which seemed to me mere exercises for poems I hadn't written. The book was praised, however, for its "gracefulness"; I had a marriage and a child. If there were doubts, if there were periods of null depression or active despairing, these could only mean that I was ungrateful, insatiable, perhaps a monster.
>
> About the time my third child was born, I felt that I had either to consider myself a failed woman and a failed poet, or to try to find some synthesis by which to understand what was happening to me.

The first step Rich took to synthesize woman and poet was to begin writing, indirectly, about the woman she had become. She acknowledges that for a poet influenced by Yeats, Dylan Thomas, and Wallace Stevens

—stylists after whom she molded her first poetry—this was a difficult decision:

> In the late fifties I was able to write, for the first time, directly about experiencing myself as a woman. The poem was jotted in fragments during children's naps, brief hours in a library, or at 3 a.m. after rising with a wakeful child. I despaired of doing any continuous work at this time. Yet I began to feel that my fragments and scraps had a common consciousness and a common theme, one which I would have been very unwilling to put on paper at an earlier time because I had been taught that poetry should be "universal," which meant, of course, non-female. Until then I had tried very much *not* to identify myself as a female poet. Over two years I wrote a 10-part poem called "Snapshots of a Daughter-in-Law," in a longer, looser mode than I'd ever trusted myself with before. It was an extraordinary relief to write that poem.

"Snapshots of a Daughter-in-Law" still holds at arm's length the central contradiction Rich was experiencing "only as suffering," in Sartre's phrase, the contradiction between her identity as homemaker and her identity as artist. Each of the ten "snapshots" portrays a different woman, *another* woman—not the poet, even when the application to Rich's own situation is obvious. One such snapshot, for example, gives us Emily Dickinson:

> Reading while waiting
> for the iron to heat,
> writing, *My Life had stood—a Loaded Gun—*
> in that Amherst pantry while the jellies boil and scum,
> or, more often,
> iron-eyed and beaked and purposed as a bird,
> dusting everything on the whatnot every day of life.

Few writers in literature have done their reading while waiting for an iron to heat or their writing in the pantry, seizing moments from other duties. But if not, why not? The significance of sexual identity dawns in poems from this period of Rich's life like the inescapable recognition of symptoms of a mortal illness. But at first she sees the problem only as a general social ill that divides the privileged from the oppressed, the safe from the endangered. In "The Roofwalker," for example, the characters who symbolize Rich's situation (and that of Denise Levertov, to whom the poem is dedicated) are still male:

The Roofwalker

—for Denise Levertov

Over the half-finished houses
night comes. The builders
stand on the roof. It is
quiet after the hammers,
the pulleys hang slack.
Giants, the roofwalkers,
on a listing deck, the wave
of darkness about to break
on their heads. The sky
is a torn sail where figures
pass magnified, shadows
on a burning deck.

I feel like them up there:
exposed, larger than life,
and due to break my neck.

Was it worth while to lay—
with infinite exertion—
a roof I can't live under?
—All those blueprints,
closing of gaps,
measurings, calculations?
A life I didn't choose
chose me: even
my tools are the wrong ones
for what I have to do.
I'm naked, ignorant,
a naked man fleeing
across the roofs
who could with a shade of difference
be sitting in the lamplight
against the cream wallpaper
reading—not with indifference—
about a naked man
fleeing across the roofs.

1961

In the line "I feel like them up there," Rich equates herself, as a

poet, with a roof-builder. The practice of their crafts renders both
"exposed . . . / and due to break [a] neck." In a second insight— the
rhetorical question "Was it worth while to lay. . . / a roof I can't live
under?"—the builder-poet dissolves into mere, terrified "naked man,"
one who can neither build roofs nor live quietly under them. Perhaps
only a housewife would find the roofline of a housing tract such a
horizon of danger. Yet in the small detail of "lamplight / against the
cream wallpaper," the poem also conveys how much at home Rich
herself has been within such rooms, reading "not with indifference"
about the naked flights of others. In short, the poem is a concise and,
for me, moving expression of the contradiction between family life
and intellectual freedom that Rich later analyzes in "When We Dead
Awaken," the essay from which I have been quoting. But in "The
Roofwalker" she has not yet arrived at the perception that eventually
comes to dominate her analysis of her own situation. "The Roofwalker"
is an important poem in Rich's history because it is one of the last in
which, when a poem needs a representative figure either of competence
or of suffering, Rich expediently uses the figure of a man.

Writing within a language, a culture, that universalizes human experience with the masculine pronoun, Rich quite logically appropriates
the symbol "naked man" as a way of expressing her experience as
universal. If she had said "naked woman," the image would not have
worked. Not until she discovers the contradiction inherent in being a
woman writing within a convention where universals are exclusively
masculine can Rich begin to control the panic she expresses in "The
Roofwalker." Then she finds that she must abandon the traditional
language that does not describe her, abandon the room with cream
wallpaper for the emptiness of a larger space beyond its lamplight.

Because the woman's half of the domestic circle is so much the arena
of Rich's most intense poetry throughout the 1960s, the last poem
that she wrote from the perspective of a wife has a special force in
the narrative of discovery recorded in her poems. Entitled "From a
Survivor," it was written the year that her estranged husband committed suicide, ending the dialogue that might have led them to new
forms of love and respect. Like time-lapse photography, the poem
condenses the beginning and end of twenty years of marriage into a
few lines.

From a Survivor

The pact that we made was the ordinary pact
of men & women in those days

I don't know who we thought we were
that our personalities
could resist the failures of the race

Lucky or unlucky, we didn't know
the race had failures of that order
and that we were going to share them

Like everybody else, we thought of ourselves as special

Your body is as vivid to me
as it ever was: even more

since my feeling for it is clearer:
I know what it could and could not do

it is no longer
the body of a god
or anything with power over my life

Next year it would have been 20 years
and you are wastefully dead
who might have made the leap
we talked, too late, of making

which I live now
not as a leap
but a succession of brief, amazing movements

each one making possible the next

1972

Her retrospective vision here both forgives and rebukes the dead man. Entering their pact was entering a condemned building. But from Rich's point of view, death was the least imaginative leap into the unknown that might have been made from the collapsing structure.

An Emerging Identity

Clearly, Rich is thinking of the "leap of faith" that Kierkegaard saw as the authentic response to a life situation in which despair is the alternative. The situation Kierkegaard formulated in *Either/Or* occurs only for those committed to mindfulness, who choose either an ethical existence or none at all. In the code of certain existentialists, suicide is preferable to mindlessness. Still, Rich implies, a man with her husband's intellectual gifts and social vision should have done better by the world, and she rejects his choice: "you are wastefully dead."

But what of her own alternative choice? By the time she wrote "From a Survivor" in 1972, Rich's passage into a new and thoroughly feminist consciousness was complete. As she remarks in "When We Dead Awaken," "The awakening of consciousness is not like the crossing of a frontier—one step, and you are in another country" (a truth evident in her own evolution), but "a succession of brief, amazing movements / each one making possible the next." Viewed in retrospect, however, these movements plot a fairly smooth curve over the years from 1968 to the present. Like a character in one of Ovid's *Metamorphoses,* Rich is disassembled and re-formed, during these years, in the pages of her books. In her poetry from 1968 to 1970 she does not know to what end the change is taking her, only that change is certain. At this stage, she writes in "Images for Godard," "the moment of change is the only poem."

When an old identity dissolves and a new one begins to emerge, Rich feels emptied of all her humanity, all the qualities that made her recognizable to those who love her:

> I am gliding backward away from those who knew me
> as the moon grows thinner and finally shuts its lantern.
> I can be replaced a thousand times,
> a box containing death.
> When you put out your hand to touch me
> you are already reaching toward an empty space.
>
> —from "Moth Hour"

For a time, Rich views this dissolution as a merely natural process, occurring in the course of a change of season:

> You're what the autumn knew would happen
> after the last collapse
> of primary color
> once the last absolutes were torn to pieces
> you could begin
>
> How you broke open, what sheathed you
> until this moment
> I know nothing about it

> my ignorance of you amazes me
> now that I watch you
> starting to give yourself away
> to the wind

from "November-1968"

Here the newborn identity is still unknown, borderless as the wind, which in poetry since the Greeks has been an archetypal symbol for the spirit. Further, this emerging identity is endowed with a consciousness hidden from the present speaker; called "you," it is viewed from the outside, and wonderingly. Nonetheless the definitive difference is apparent: in poems written between 1968 and 1971 that spiritual power had become anchored in *female* forms. The poem "Planetarium" (1968) describes one such definitive anchoring, in which she perceives power first as female and then as hers:

Planetarium

Thinking of Caroline Herschel (1750-1848)
astronomer, sister of William; and others.

A woman in the shape of a monster
a monster in the shape of a woman
the skies are full of them

a woman   'in the snow
among the Clocks and instruments
or measuring the ground with poles'
in her 98 years to discover
8 comets

she whom the moon ruled
like us
levitating into the night sky
riding the polished lenses

Galaxies of women, there
doing penance for impetuousness
ribs chilled
in those spaces   of the mind

An eye,

          'virile, precise and absolutely certain'
          from the mad webs of Uranusborg
                              encountering the NOVA

every impulse of light exploding
from the core
as life flies out of us

      Tycho whispering at last
      'Let me not seem to have lived in vain'

What we see, we see
and seeing is changing

the light that shrivels a mountain
and leaves a man alive

Heartbeat of the pulsar
heart sweating through my body

The radio impulse
pouring in from Taurus

      I am bombarded yet   I stand

I have been standing all my life in the
direct path of a battery of signals
the most accurately transmitted most
untranslatable language in the universe
I am a galactic cloud so deep   so invo-
luted that a light wave could take 15
years to travel through me   And has
taken   I am an instrument in the shape
of a woman trying to translate pulsations
into images   for the relief of the body
and the reconstruction of the mind.

1968

Breaking the Hold of the Past

After 1970 Rich's intuition of her power and the work she might do, as glimpsed in "Planetarium," has become a reality, and she writes from the center of a well-defined political goal. She describes that goal in "When We Dead Awaken":

      Re-vision—the act of looking back, of seeing with
    fresh eyes, of entering an old text from a new critical direc-

tion—is for us more than a chapter in cultural history: it is an act of survival. Until we can understand the assumptions in which we are drenched we cannot know ourselves. And this drive to self-knowledge, for woman, is more than a search for identity: it is part of her refusal of the self-destructiveness of male-dominated society. A radical critique of literature, feminist in its impulse, would take the work first of all as a clue to how we live, how we have been living, how we have been led to imagine ourselves, how our language has trapped as well as liberated us; and how we can begin to see—and therefore live—afresh. A change in the concept of sexual identity is essential if we are not going to see the old political order re-assert itself in every new revolution. We need to know the writing of the past, and know it differently than we have ever known it; not to pass on a tradition but to break its hold over us.

This paragraph names the two tasks Rich, "survivor" of a "chapter in cultural history," has singled out as worth devoting her life to helping accomplish. One is the project of being a woman; the other is the project of being a writer. They blend in her will to assert herself against the "self-destructiveness"—personal and social—"of male-dominated society" through the use of tools that in 1961, in "The Roofwalker," had seemed "the wrong ones / for what I have to do." Rich has passed through a period of severe doubt that many poets undergo, questioning whether writing poetry can be regarded as valuable work. Those who survive as poets often do so, as Rich has done, by changing their relationship to their art. In Rich's case this has meant seeing with fresh eyes the content of her own metaphors—for example, that in which the poet (by inference, male) is a builder of roofs under which a reader reads in safe detachment. In her poems now Rich is no longer passing on a tradition but breaking its hold: "the words are purposes. / The words are maps."

In requoting these lines I have come full circle from my first paragraphs on Rich. Rich's poems create a context for each other: to be fully understood they should be read in large numbers and in chronological order. "Snapshots of a Daughter-in-Law," "The Roofwalker," "Planetarium," "From a Survivor," and "Translations" can be understood as scenes in a drama that has unfolded over time, a drama of conversion in which a mature and talented woman comes under the influence of a vision so compelling that it cannot be set aside: it changes her life.

"which I live now
not as a leap
but a succession of brief, amazing movements

each one making possible the next"

Yet Rich's writing is not merely personal and autobiographical. One of her motives in writing has been her observation that her experience is not exceptional. Another is her observation that, by disclosing realities, art changes them. Hence, in her poetry since 1971 Rich has been trying to mirror women not only as they are, but as they have not been seen. This is not an easy task. Her obvious problem is to find or imagine symbolic figures with the kinds of social meanings the builder so usefully supplies in the symbolism of "The Roofwalker." The tradition, especially the poetic tradition, of a male-dominated culture offers little help. Thus, like other contemporary women poets, Rich has sought subjects in a countertradition of histories and mythologies of powerful women, as well as in the common life she shares with women around her. She has been prolific, and she has not always been mindful enough, as she acknowledges in a poem from her most recent book, *The Dream of a Common Language:*

> There are words I cannot choose again:
> *humanism   androgyny*
>
> Such words have no shame in them, no diffidence
> before the raging stoic grandmothers:
>
> their glint is too shallow, like a dye
> that does not permeate
>
> the fibers of actual life
> as we live it, now:
>
> this fraying blanket with its ancient stains
> we pull across the sick child's shoulder
>
> or wrap around the senseless legs
> of the hero trained to kill
>
> this weaving, ragged because incomplete
> we turn our hands to, interrupted
>
> over and over, handed down
> unfinished, found in the drawer
>
> of an old dresser in the barn,
> her vanished pride and care

still urging us, urging on
our work, to close the gap

in the Great Nebula,
to help the earth deliver.

—from "Natural Resources"

Even this poem is damaged by the abstractness it disowns, reaching as it does for a cosmic rationale, an elevating idea with which to close. Yet the image of weaving that has been handed down through generations of women as a piece of unfinished work is a metaphor expressive of Rich's profound belief in poetry and all other arts. Rich regards women's art not as decorative but as useful, essentially so—an extension of their capacities for caring, nurturing. As in Mary Cassatt's painting, where the woman's lap and arms support the little girl as she looks into a mirror, Rich's art seeks to convey the responsibility of one woman for another in terms of how lovingly one woman can help another to see herself.

"The river turns on itself,
The tree retreats into its own shadow
I feel a weightless change, a moving forward
As of water quickening before a narrowing channel"

CHAPTER FIVE

Renewed by Death:
Poetry of Theodore Roethke

Midway in the journey of our life I came to myself in a dark wood where the straight road was lost.

Ah, how hard it is to tell what a wild, and rough, and stubborn wood this was: the very thought of it renews the fear!

So bitter is it, that death is scarcely more so; but to treat of the good that I found in it, I will tell of all the other things I saw.

Dante, from Inferno of The Divine Comedy

"MIDWAY IN THE JOURNEY of our life I came to myself in a dark wood," begins Dante's *Inferno*. In many editions of this poem a footnote follows the phrase "midway in the journey of our life," pointing out that the narrator is thirty-five when the events in the poem occur—halfway through the allotment of years composing a human life, according to the Book of Psalms. Awareness of his mortality has seared Dante's consciousness, thrusting him into the state of dread with which the poem starkly opens.

"The straight road was lost" because it never existed. Man and woman pass from birth to death only once; their paths appear only behind them, as evidence of their passage. This recognition makes life seem like a wilderness. Even the thought of that dark place renews fear, Dante says, and is so bitter "that death is scarcely more so." Yet the realization also brings the narrator to *himself,* as one is said to be "brought to" from a state of unconsciousness. Shedding the habits, comforts, and evasions of thirty-five years, he passes through the circles of hell, where in hundreds of forms he confronts the specters of human limitation, but he emerges from this trial with renewed faith in his life's meaning. It is "to treat of the good" found in his terror and dread that he undertakes the poem.

Dante's world has long since vanished, and the political and religious structures that for him embodied ideals of human order have undergone several revolutions since the completion of *The Divine Comedy.* Yet Dante's hero—the individual accosted by his mortality and made to answer for his life, the self capable of being awakened within us out of the slumberous habits of normal consciousness—is an archetype as meaningful today as then. Eternity surrounds us, pressing on our consciousness with what Wordsworth described as the sound of "mighty waters, rolling evermore." The shoreline where the human eye encounters a limitless void is the vista of the poetry of death, poetry inspired by the recognition that life is very short and that in our day-to-day existence death is a constant presence. Sometimes this awareness arrives after a sudden bereavement, but more often it reveals itself less perceptibly, as in an unintentional glimpse in a mirror. However the vista of death confronts our startled eyes, at whatever time of life, it imposes a vision that we can either attempt to deny or build upon through acceptance.

Different ages produce different philosophies to counter the anguish of the knowledge of mortality. But the anguish itself has been a theme in poetry of the Western tradition from classical and biblical times to the present. In modern American poetry, no writer has made this theme more significantly a subject than has Theodore Roethke (1908-63) in a group of long poems entitled *North American Sequence.* Like Dante, Roethke explores the horror of his own mortality in order to live the remainder of his life more conscious of its meaning.

The Poet's Craft

Roethke has written about the relation between his life and his poetry in a number of personal statements gathered posthumously into a book entitled *On the Poet and His Craft.* An experimentalist in art who wished his experiments to be understood, Roethke felt he had to prepare his readers for encounters they would make with potentially mystifying word structures. One particularly helpful gloss on the biographical references in *North American Sequence* appears in "An American Poet Introduces Himself and His Poems," originally a talk delivered over BBC radio. There Roethke describes his family background and his childhood home, both central to his project as a poet:

> Everyone knows that America is a continent, but few Europeans realize the various and diverse parts of this land. The Saginaw Valley, where I was born, had been great lumbering country in the 1880's. It is very fertile flat country in Michigan, and the principal towns, Saginaw and Flint, lie at the northern edge of what is now the central industrial area of the United States.
>
> It was to this region that my grandfather came in 1870 from Prussia, where he had been Bismarck's head forester. He and his sons started some greenhouses which became the most extensive in that part of America.
>
> It was a wonderful place for a child to grow up in and around. There were not only twenty-five acres in the town, mostly under glass and intensely cultivated, but farther out in the country the last stand of virgin timber in the Saginaw Valley and, elsewhere, a wild area of cut-over second-growth timber, which my father and uncle made into a small game preserve.

In attempting to identify himself simply and concisely to a foreign audience, Roethke begins with place rather than with genealogy. He names a locale, and he characterizes his ancestors in terms of the traits they embodied. The Prussian forester who brought his sons from the Old World to the newly settled Saginaw Valley brought also a tradition of overseeing nature. When Roethke's grandfather arrived, he transformed a wilderness into a world. With Prussian efficiency he made decisions about how nature should function for him, setting twenty-five acres under glass to cultivate and appointing other uses to the rest. Wilderness became "preserve." His sons and their wives consolidated the lands under family control, so that greenhouse and wilderness, "forcing house" and "far field," became the poles of Theodore Roethke's world as a child and, metaphorically, the existential poles of his poetry:

> What the greenhouses themselves were to me I try to indicate in my second book, *The Lost Son and Other Poems*. . . .
> They were to me, I realize now, both heaven and hell, a kind

of tropics created in the savage climate of Michigan, where austere German-Americans turned their love of order and their terrifying efficiency into something truly beautiful. It was a universe, several worlds, which, even as a child, one worried about, and struggled to keep alive.

A world can be distinguished from mere nature; it is space created within nature by human will and imagination, to support life according to a design. The world composed by Roethke's grandfather, father, and uncle was created almost in defiance of nature: an alternative world, with its own seasons, wrested out of virgin land and protected from a savage climate. This relation to nature became a controlling paradigm in Roethke's art: that the human role in nature is to shape a habitation for oneself within this wilderness, through the exercise of imagination and energy, by appointing functions and establishing limits. The world that emerges from these fiats contains both a heaven and a hell—and it is easily destroyed.

Out of this line of terrifying gardeners, then, came a man destined to cultivate not plants but language. Roethke began composing poetry as an avocation in college. After a brief stint at law school he turned to graduate study at Michigan and Harvard in English literature. The Depression interrupted his work before he received a Ph.D., but in 1931 he found a job and began his career in college teaching. In 1947 he became a professor at the University of Washington, where he remained until his death in 1963. The Pacific Northwest is the main source of symbolic geography in *North American Sequence*.

For Roethke, teaching poetry and writing it were complementary activities, partly because of the large circle of acquaintances he developed outside the university among working poets who gave him hardheaded criticism—lean on theory and heavy on practical advice. Roethke taught his students with the same spirit in which he sought criticism, regarding all practicing poets as laborers mastering a trade. His essays on the craft of poetry—"The Teaching Poet" and "How to Write Like Somebody Else"—make invaluable handbooks for teachers and practitioners alike.

Roethke's career as a poet, as distinct from his career as a professor, had three clearly delineated stages, each culminating in the publication of collected poems—in 1941, 1958, and 1963. His earliest poetry (1925-41) was highly polished, formal, and impersonal in subject matter. An influential model for Roethke when he began writing was W.H. Auden, who believed that the mark of authenticity in a poet was the ability to work in any verse form—to speak in a tongue not one's own, loyal to form itself. In Roethke's early poetry, subject matter is a secondary concern, subsumed within the larger goal of writing all kinds of poems. Every poet writes from experience, but the formative experiences of a poet often occur while reading, which consumes much of a poet's time. Accordingly, the poet takes subjects from books as easily as from daily life. That an experience has already been handled in a poem often makes it easier for another poet to find it a desirable subject for a poem of his or her own. Not surprisingly, then, the poems in Roethke's first book, *Open House* (1941), though well made, are traditional and rather obviously imitative of poets he admired.

A definitive change in Roethke's art was the emergence after 1941 of a highly personal subject matter, derived from recurring psychotic episodes, variously diagnosed as "manic depressive" and "paranoid schizophrenic," for which he continued to be hospitalized throughout his life. These episodes seriously disrupted his teaching and his friendships, but they did not disrupt the flow of poetry. As Roethke's biographer Allan Seager remarks in *The Glass House,* "Well or ill, he wrote poetry or took notes for poetry nearly every day of his adult life. Poetry was the central fact of his life, and everything else . . . clung to it like filings to a magnet."

Roethke's illnesses appear, in fact, to have opened new paths into consciousness. Humbled and instructed by the terrors of mental disintegration and self-confrontation, he evolved new modes of expression for them. The poems in *The Lost Son and Other Poems* (1948) and *Praise to the End!* (1951), books from the second phase of his development as an artist, record repeated spiritual journeys from helplessness to coherence. The poems are written in a style Roethke called "psychic shorthand." Almost any passage from these sequences supplies a good example of this style:

> Bullheads have whiskers.
> And they bite.

> He watered the roses.
> His thumb had a rainbow.
> The stems said, Thank you.
> Dark came early.

> That was before. I fell! I fell!
> The worm has moved away.
> My tears are tired.
> —from "Where Knock Is Open Wide"

The imagery reflects a child's complex responses to his father's power—the terror and the gratitude it inspires—viewed helplessly from the perspective of an adult's psychotic breakdown: "I fell! I fell!" The adult relives the child's intuition that his father's power is somehow expressed by his penis. Bullhead, thumb, stems, worms—all the phallic-shaped objects of vision—have come to symbolize this mysterious fatherly power, and occur in the poem as in the tormented mind, side by side, without explanatory connectives. Roethke was proud of his poetic shorthand, despite the difficulties it offered the reader. In "Open Letter" he explains, "If intensity has compressed the language so it seems, on early reading, obscure, this obscurity should break open suddenly for the serious reader who can hear the language: the 'meaning' itself should come as a dramatic revelation, an excitement."

In the third and final phase of his development as a writer (1958-63), Roethke reaped benefits from both preceding stages: the discipline of his formalism yielded him range, and the mastery of his most compelling subject, himself, gave him the confidence to pursue the theme of loss and recapture of his own spiritual wholeness. *Words for the Wind* (1958) won Roethke the Pulitzer Prize. But his last book, *The Far Field* (which appeared posthumously) contains what I regard as his finest work, *North American Sequence*. These are six poems Roethke worked on for several years and published one by one between 1959 and 1963: "The Longing," "Meditation at Oyster River," "Journey to the Interior," "The Long Waters," "The Far Field," and "The Rose." He considered each poem to be comprehensible on its own terms. Yet, read as a sequence, the poems initiate and resolve a subject larger than any treated individually. They form a spiritual autobiography that extends in time and space from childhood to mid-life, from Saginaw, Michigan, west across the continent to Puget Sound, Washington; and in a spiritual dimension from the dark confinement of a narrow egotism at the opening of the first poem ("The Longing") to a beach where a self rests "rooted in stone, keeping the whole of light" ("The Rose"). Roethke's earlier sequences of poems had treated, in biographical order, first the child's passage into adolescence *(The Lost Son)*, which chronicles a reacquisition of trust in the self; then the time of life when the solitary adult learns with fearful joy to embrace another human being in sexual love *(Words for the Wind)*. In *North American Sequence* Roethke explores mortality; like Dante, he composes a face to confront the face that death raises in his path: the face of a "final man" at peace "in a place leading nowhere."

North American Sequence: The Challenge of Death

The self persists like a dying star,
In sleep, afraid. Death's face rises afresh,
Among the shy beasts, the deer at the salt-lick,
The doe with its sloped shoulders loping across the highway,
The young snake, poised in green leaves, waiting for its fly,
The hummingbird, whirring from quince-blossom to morning-glory—
With these I would be.

And with water: the waves coming forward, without cessation,
The waves, altered by sand-bars, beds of kelp, miscellaneous
    driftwood,
Topped by cross-winds, tugged at by sinuous undercurrents,
The tide rustling in, sliding between the ridges of stone,
The tongues of water, creeping in, quietly.

—from "Meditation at Oyster River"

I, who came back from the depths laughing too loudly,
Become another thing;
My eyes extend beyond the farthest bloom of the waves;
I lose and find myself in the long water;
I am gathered together once more;
I embrace the world.

—from "The Long Waters"

The lines quoted above from the second and fourth poems of *North American Sequence* identify the anxiety explored in the sequence as a whole: the fear of death and the desire to compose, before extinction, a spirit so in accord with reality that it may embrace mortality itself as a precious aspect of the world's being.

Roethke was fifty-one and in reasonably good health when he began writing *North American Sequence*. Though he was to die suddenly of a coronary occlusion, while preparing for publication what turned out to be his last book, Roethke did not write these poems knowing death was imminent. Rather, he had undergone an experience common in middle age. As psychiatrist Erik Erikson has observed, middle age is a time when the individual struggles to achieve a sense of integrity within a context of growing disgust and despair: disgust at the aging body and its failing powers, despair that time is short and that most of one's choices for better or worse have already been made. These precisely are the characteristics of Roethke's situation in the opening lines of *North American Sequence:*

> On things asleep, no balm:
> A kingdom of stinks and sighs,
> Fetor of cockroaches, dead fish, petroleum,
> Worse than castoreum of mink or weasels,
> Saliva dripping from warm microphones,
> Agony of crucifixion on barstools.
> . . . .
> Lust fatigues the soul.
> How to transcend this sensual emptiness?
> (Dreams drain the spirit if we dream too long.)
> In a bleak time, when a week of rain is a year,
> The slag-heaps fume at the edge of the raw cities:
> The gulls wheel over their singular garbage;
> The great trees no longer shimmer
> Not even the soot dances.
>
> And the spirit fails to move forward,
> But shrinks into a half-life, less than itself,
> Falls back, a slug, a loose worm
> Ready for any crevice,
> An eyeless starer.
>
> —from "The Longing"

The setting for the onset of Roethke's longing is, aptly, an urban wasteland: not Dante's trackless wood but Eliot's Unreal City (of *The Waste Land*). As the work of Elizabeth Kubler-Ross and other psychotherapists who treat terminally ill patients indicates, social evolution has made death more difficult to face in modern life than in the past, when the ill and the aged were more likely to spend their last days in the surroundings of family life. "Dying nowadays is more gruesome in many ways," Kubler-Ross observes in *On Death and Dying*. Given over into the hands of technicians, the patient, worn and helpless, may cry for rest, peace, and dignity, but he will get infusions, transfusions, a heart machine, or tracheotomy if necessary. He may want one single person to stop for one single minute so that he can ask one single question—but he will get a dozen people around the clock, all busily preoccupied with his heart rate, pulse, electrocardiogram or pulmonary functions, his secretions or excretions but not with him as a human being. He may wish to fight it all but it is going to be a useless fight since all this is done in the fight for his life, and if they can save his life they can consider the person afterwards. Those who consider the person first may lose precious time to save his life!

Kubler-Ross began her work with the dying to help individual patients attain peace and dignity and also, by initiating seminars on death and dying, to provide doctors with a perspective ignored in their medical training: that the dying body is a human being. Kubler-Ross saw the doctors' denial of death—reluctance to give a patient a diagnosis that illness was terminal, extravagant efforts to prolong life in the sheerly technical sense, and other kinds of avoidance—as a manifestation of the general tendency of human beings to deny their own mortality, an attitude shared by doctors and patients alike. But Kubler-Ross observed that among dying patients denial was usually a temporary phase, followed by anger, then bargaining for a better deal, then grief and depression, and finally—beyond the hope of reprieve—acceptance. "So here it is at last, the distinguished thing," novelist Henry James reportedly said on his deathbed. Such acceptance offers a model of the "good death" to all of us, dying every moment at our own pace.

North American Sequence is about the process of achieving this final serene relation to death. In these poems Roethke is beyond denial, beyond bargaining, beyond anger, and almost beyond grief. He is ready to make his peace with the world. Each of the poems in the sequence reenacts a movement of the psyche from anguish to acceptance. In each, the poet reconsiders, with utmost attentiveness, his kinship with the myriad lives around him. In the lines quoted from "Meditation at Oyster River," for example, these are the lives of certain "shy beasts." Deer, snake, fly, hummingbird—to some extent even quince-blossom and morning-glory—represent forms of life simpler than his own: mortal, like him, but unconscious of their mortality. "With these I would be"—this desire, in Roethke, is the initial stage of surrender of the ego, creating space for passage to a higher level of spiritual integration. "I believe that to go forward as a spiritual man it is necessary first to go back," Roethke says. By going back he means not only into personal history—the path of psychoanalysis—but also into evolutionary history, to recover the unity of self and world in their common source, the slime of primordial matter.

> If the dead can come to our aid in a quest for identity, so can the living—and I mean *all* living things, including the sub-human. . . . It is paradoxical that a very sharp sense of the being, the identity of some other being—and in some instances, even an inanimate thing—brings a corresponding heightening and awareness of one's own self, *and,* even more mysteriously, in some instances, a feeling of the oneness of the universe. . . . If you can effect this, then you are by way of getting somewhere: knowing you will break from self-involvement.
>
> —from "On 'Identity'"

"With these I would be. And with water," he writes in "Meditation at Oyster River." To empty the self and then dissolve its structure are the first creative acts he deploys under the pressure of his will to change. Moving "forward, without cessation," water is symbolic of the imaginative process, the agent of regeneration and reconciliation. This symbolism is brought to culmination in the closing lines of "The Far Field," where the poet's peaceful self-containment—"the pure serene of memory in one man"—embraces all of nature, "winding around the waters of the world."

As the lines quoted from "Meditation at Oyster River" and "The Long Waters" indicate, Roethke's style in *North American Sequence* is limpid and plain, the syntax as straightforward as it might be in prose. Above all, his language is concrete. Roethke uses few abstractions in these poems; when a metaphysical term such as "spirit" appears, its meaning is familiar. The realism of Roethke's art here is one aspect of its beauty, as realism is an aspect of the beauty in paintings by Andrew Wyeth. Presented with imagery so true to life, however, the reader may tend to overlook its intellectual components, the principles governing the selection of details such as his symbolic use of flowing water in the passages quoted above. At every point in these lines Roethke is referring not only to the movement of the incoming tide in an actual place, named in the title, but also to the movement of the mind as it touches, with sinuous undercurrents of thought, the objects in a field of perception—surrounding, embracing, and finally giving voice to them.

The shape of Roethke's lines in these poems is equally significant. Each line completes a unit of syntax: no preposition is sundered from its object, no adjective from its noun. The free verse of these poems would seem to be the simplest form of poetic freedom, verging on the relative formlessness of prose. Yet it is deliberate and designed. The characteristic appearance of the verse reflects the expanding and contracting of thought—a visual printout of the flow and ebb of mental energy.

The challenge death presents to Roethke in the poems of *North American Sequence,* then, is twofold. It is a challenge to Roethke's humanity, his ability to overcome anxiety and transcend denial; it is equally a challenge to his art. Roethke works in this poem to recreate in words the processes of mind that transform fear into wisdom. This is the spiritual project accomplished in the central poem of *North American Sequence,* "The Far Field."

The Far Field

I

I dream of journeys repeatedly:
Of flying like a bat deep into a narrowing tunnel,
Of driving alone, without luggage, out a long peninsula,
The road lined with snow-laden second growth,
A fine dry snow ticking the windshield,
Alternate snow and sleet, no on-coming traffic,
And no lights behind, in the blurred side-mirror,
The road changing from glazed tarface to a rubble of stone,
Ending at last in a hopeless sand-rut,
Where the car stalls,
Churning in a snowdrift
Until the headlights darken.

II

At the field's end, in the corner missed by the mower,
Where the turf drops off into a grass-hidden culvert,
Haunt of the cat-bird, nesting-place of the field-mouse,
Not too far away from the ever-changing flower-dump,
Among the tin cans, tires, rusted pipes, broken machinery,—
One learned of the eternal;
And in the shrunken face of a dead rat, eaten by rain and ground-
     beetles
(I found it lying among the rubble of an old coal bin)
And the tom-cat, caught near the pheasant-run,
Its entrails strewn over the half-grown flowers,
Blasted to death by the night watchman.

I suffered for birds, for young rabbits caught in the mower,
My grief was not excessive.

For to come upon warblers in early May
Was to forget time and death:
How they filled the oriole's elm, a twittering restless cloud, all one
    morning,
And I watched and watched till my eyes blurred from the bird
    shapes,—
Cape May, Blackburnian, Cerulean,—
Moving, elusive as fish, fearless,
Hanging, bunched like young fruit, bending the end branches,
Still for a moment,
Then pitching away in half-flight,
Lighter than finches,
While the wrens bickered and sang in the half-green hedgerows,
And the flicker drummed from his dead tree in the chicken-yard.

—Or to lie naked in sand,
In the silted shallows of a slow river,
Fingering a shell,
Thinking:
Once I was something like this, mindless,
Or perhaps with another mind, less peculiar;
Or to sink down to the hips in a mossy quagmire;
Or, with skinny knees, to sit astride a wet log,
Believing:
I'll return again,
As a snake or a raucous bird,
Or, with luck, as a lion.

I learned not to fear infinity,
The far field, the windy cliffs of forever,
The dying of time in the white light of tomorrow,
The wheel turning away from itself,
The sprawl of the wave,
The on-coming water.

III

The river turns on itself,
The tree retreats into its own shadow.
I feel a weightless change, a moving forward
As of water quickening before a narrowing channel
When banks converge, and the wide river whitens;
Or when two rivers combine, the blue glacial torrent
And the yellowish-green from the mountainy upland,—
At first a swift rippling between rocks,

Then a long running over flat stones
Before descending to the alluvial plain,
To the clay banks, and the wild grapes hanging from the elmtrees.
The slightly trembling water
Dropping a fine yellow silt where the sun stays;
And the crabs bask near the edge,
The weedy edge, alive with small snakes and bloodsuckers,—

I have come to a still, but not a deep center,
A point outside the glittering current;
My eyes stare at the bottom of a river,
At the irregular stones, irridescent sandgrains,
My mind moves in more than one place,
In a country half-land, half-water.

I am renewed by death, thought of my death,
The dry scent of a dying garden in September,
The wind fanning the ash of a low fire.
What I love is near at hand,
Always, in earth and air.

IV

The lost self changes,
Turning toward the sea,
A sea-shape turning around,—
An old man with his feet before the fire,
In robes of green, in garments of adieu.

A man faced with his own immensity
Wakes all the waves, all their loose wandering fire.
The murmur of the absolute, the why
Of being born fails on his naked ears.
His spirit moves like monumental wind
That gentles on a sunny blue plateau.
He is the end of things, the final man.

All finite things reveal infinitude:
The mountain with its singular bright shade
Like the blue shine on freshly frozen snow,
The after-light upon ice-burdened pines;
Odor of basswood on a mountain-slope,
A scent beloved of bees;
Silence of water above a sunken tree:
The pure serene of memory in one man,—
A ripple widening from a single stone
Winding around the waters of the world.

    "The Far Field" is divided into four parts; but why? No subtitles or transitions provide the reader with interpretive cues. Yet the poem has shape, the way a sonnet has shape. "The Far Field" may be described as a *meditative lyric,* a poetic form used by many poets when dealing with subjects of great personal and philosophical significance—William Wordsworth in "Tintern Abbey," T.S. Eliot in *Four Quartets,* Wallace Stevens in "The Idea of Order at Key West," to name only a few.
    The meditative poem opens with the poet focusing his thoughts, in a very specific setting, on a significant problem—such as the fear of death, the subject of section I of "The Far Field." Then the poet scrutinizes the problem, using all his powers of memory, will, and understanding. Memory recovers moments from the past when the poet was able to contend successfully with the problem at hand; will keeps him determined not to deny reality or be deluded by falsifications; understanding enables him to distinguish between false and true. In "The Far Field" these analytical processes occupy sections II and III. Finally, having arrived at some kind of resolution, the poet ends the meditative

poem in a mood of praise. Like Jacob wrestling with the angel in the Book of Genesis, the poet has won a blessing from his struggle and now knows his own strength.

The meditative structure, however, is only one form of organization in "The Far Field." Another structure of equal importance is provided by interplay between two kinds of vision, associated with what I shall describe as the *horizontal plane* and the *vertical axis* of imagery in the poem. The horizontal plane is that of *process*—the flow of time bearing us constantly toward our deaths. The vertical axis is *consciousness,* which, rising at any point out of the horizontal, attains perspective and beholds the events of the horizontal as components of a pattern, rather than as a flow. From the vantage point of the vertical axis, a life becomes a story, with a beginning, middle, and end.

The qualities associated with the horizontal are the blind, irreversible movements of things toward extinction:

> Of flying like a bat deep into a narrowing tunnel,
> . . . .
> Churning in a snowdrift
> Until the headlights darken.
> . . . .
> The wheel turning away from itself,
> The sprawl of the wave,
> The on-coming water.

Associated with the vertical are all things elevated and airborne: the eyes, sounds, scents, and the human spirit moving free as wind upon the face of the waters until at last it "gentles on a sunny blue plateau." This interplay of horizontal and vertical, however, is present not as sterile abstraction but rather as an insight into the real world that becomes symbolic in the course of the poem's unfolding section by section.

Section I: "The headlights darken"

The opening of "The Far Field" presents a nightmare vision of a certain horrible kind of death—the kind that comes on swiftly, giving one time for consciousness of its approach, but little time to prepare one's soul:

> I dream of journeys repeatedly:
> Of flying like a bat deep into a narrowing tunnel,
> Of driving alone, without luggage, out a long peninsula,
> The road lined with snow-laden second growth,
> A fine dry snow ticking the windshield,

> Alternate snow and sleet, no on-coming traffic,
> And no lights behind, in the blurred side-mirror,
> The road changing from glazed tarface to a rubble of stone,
> Ending at last in a hopeless sand-rut,
> Where the car stalls,
> Churning in a snowdrift
> Until the headlights darken.

Roethke's own death of a heart attack while swimming may have contained a few moments of such terror. Yet this dread is not reserved only for those within minutes of dying. The lines record a depressive fantasy that can come easily in mid-life as a consequence of a sense of being at a dead end, with energies failing. And the rhythmic structure of the lines provides subliminal support for this imagery of entropy; the whole section is one long sentence, with a spinal column of participles—flying, driving, ticking, on-coming, changing, ending, churning—that terminates in the strong active verb, darken.

Darkness is a common poetic symbol for dread; Dante, for example, uses a dark wood as the setting for his own confrontation with mortality at the opening of *Inferno*. In Roethke's poem as in Dante's, darkness does not signify fear of death so much as fear of meaninglessness: the fantasy of "driving alone . . . / Until the headlights darken" implies a gradual but total abnegation of the self's resources for survival. The darkening headlights suggest the darkened head of a self who has become a blind system of organic processes, without imagination or will—a mere mechanism, a mere body.

This frightful repeated dream of meaninglessness poses a question to the poet: What alternatives can you find, within yourself, to dying in this manner, like a road running out or a battery fading? The next two sections form the poet's response. In them he ascends from the nightmare horizontal plane of tunnel and sand-rut to a perspective that integrates past, present, and future and allows him to formulate a heroic answer to fear.

Section II: "I learned not to fear infinity"

Because his concern is a loss of meaning, the poet begins by retracing his steps, going back to the time and place where he first "learned of the eternal"—and learned not to fear it. Most of us do not remember acquiring such knowledge; it seems, from the vantage point of adulthood, one of the things we have always known. Yet psychiatrists who study children find that the discovery of death occurs very early and that death is a pervasive concern for a child. In *Existential Psychotherapy*, psychiatrist Irving Yalom of Stanford describes his clinical experiences with the poignancy of the child's complicated accommodations to the idea of death:

> The child at a very early age stumbles upon the "true facts of life"—perhaps his silent researches lead him to the discovery of death. But it is too much to face, he is overwhelmed by his discovery and experiences naked anxiety and its attendants—nightmares, night terrors, phobias. Though he searches for reassurance he must deal with death: he may panic in the face of it, deny it, personify it, scoff at it, repress it, but deal with it he must. Finally during "latency" he learns (or is taught) to negate reality. Gradually as he develops efficient and sophisticated forms of denial the awareness of death glides into the unconscious and the explicit fear of death abates. . . . During adolescence, childhood denial systems are no longer effective. The introspective tendencies and the greater resources of the adolescent permit him to face, once again, the awareness of death, to bear the anxiety and to search for alternate modes of coping with the facts of life.

This early drama of discovery, denial, and acceptance is the theme of section II of "The Far Field." But as a poet Roethke has motives that go beyond mere accurate notation of his personal case history. For Roethke perceives that he owes the success of his earliest dealings with anxiety about death to the power of his imagination, the power that enabled him eventually to become a poet.

Section II of "The Far Field" is, for me, one of the most beautiful things Roethke ever made. It is a poem-within-a-poem, composed of four parts whose themes may be briefly stated:

> I learned of the eternal;
> I suffered, I forgot;
> I thought, I believed;
> I learned not to fear.

Each typographical separation in section I indicates a development of consciousness. The first part describes the child's earliest encounters with death, during what Yalom refers to as those "silent researches" children perform in hidden corners or, as Roethke says, "at the field's end." The first lines zoom in on the scene of discovery with the deliberate movement of a documentary camera: "the shrunken face of a dead rat, eaten by rain and ground-beetles," "entrails strewn over the half-grown flowers." Here we get a good look at death, that we may share the child's need to learn not to fear it. Death is commonplace and dreadful in these lines.

However, the language of this first stanza of section II is detached, unemotional, and precise: *one* learned of the eternal *at* this place and *in* these sights; death has merely been discovered as a fact. What the child does with his discovery fills the next two parts of this section. First, he turns his eyes elsewhere:

> I suffered for birds, for young rabbits caught in the mower,
> My grief was not excessive.
> For to come upon warblers in early May
> Was to forget time and death.

On an initial reading, these lines may seem to describe the child's simplest and most predictable act of denial: think about something pleasant and death will go away. Yet the lines that follow convey an ecstatic energy that insists something more complicated and more positive is happening in the child's mind:

> And I watched and watched till my eyes blurred from the bird shapes,—
> Cape May, Blackburnian, Cerulean,—
> Moving, elusive as fish, fearless,
> Hanging, bunched like young fruit, bending the end branches,
> Still for a moment,
> Then pitching away in half-flight,
> Lighter than finches,
> While the wrens bickered and sang in the half-green hedgerows,
> And the flicker drummed from his dead tree in the chicken-yard.

The child "forgets" time and death because his mind is totally occupied with the moment; whatever fills his field of vision engages his complete attention. The child, watching and watching, is caught up in the kind of rapt and blissful seeing that Wordsworth in "Intimations of Immortality" calls primal sympathy, "the fountain light . . . of all our seeing," when the world presents itself to our eyes with all "the glory and the freshness of a dream." The child in Roethke's lines, however, has already achieved a certain cognitive sophistication. He is not merely a passive beholder of these creatures; he knows them by species and can refer to them by their proper names; moreover, he can capture them in similes. Similes enter this section of the poem only after we have entered the consciousness of the child, moving from the generalization "one learned" to the intimacy "I suffered"; for similes reflect the subjectivity of knowledge. "Moving, elusive as fish" and "hanging, bunched like young fruit" are simple metaphors, but they indicate that the child can already grasp the world in terms of abstractions and is no longer immersed in the horizontal plane as silent monitor of the world's phenomenal flow. The child's denial is a creative attentiveness to the larger world, which contains death as an aspect of life.

A slightly later stage of cognitive development is manifest in the next stanza, wherein the child draws certain facts, gleaned from a rudimentary study of evolution, into the charged field of thinking about his own death:

> Thinking:
> Once I was something like this, mindless,
> Or perhaps with another mind, less peculiar.

The idea of reincarnation also strikes him as useful:

> Believing:
> I'll return again,
> As a snake or a raucous bird,
> Or, with luck, as a lion.

Thinking, in this important existential situation, becomes an avenue to believing, as the typographical isolation of those two words indicates. We are meant to see that the child's belief here is touchingly inadequate—a form of whistling in the dark. Even so, it manifests the mind's creative power to press back against the terror of death, and not only through denial. The child's response is both more generous than denial and more adaptive: more generous in its active receptivity to the world as he finds it, teeming with conflict; more adaptive in its intelligence about the relations of things to each other and to himself. It is in like manner that each of us comes—if we do—to the state of trust expressed in the last lines:

> I learned not to fear infinity,
> The far field, the windy cliffs of forever,
> The dying of time in the white light of tomorrow,
> The wheel turning away from itself,
> The sprawl of the wave,
> The on-coming water.

Section III: "I am renewed by death, thought of my death"

The description of the growth of trust described in section II provides in section III what Wordsworth called the "fountain light" by which the present is illuminated for the adult. The imagery of flowing water, which Roethke uses to symbolize the flow of living consciousness, perpetuates the child's responsiveness within the adult's mature intelligence. The poet's history of coping with the fear of death comes to his aid now, as he detects his own death in "the dry scent of a dying garden in September," and the sight of "wind fanning the ash of a low fire." *He* is a dying garden and a dying fire. But his consciousness is more than these. It is like a great river flowing, responsive to every pressure and change, keeping its own pace, and freshening the lives it touches. The water is, in every syllable, both water—described with minute attentiveness—and a metaphor for the power of quickening consciousness to rise above itself, to move "in more than one place," from the vantage of "a point outside the glittering current," to survey its origins, its growth and change, its end. In so detaching himself from the flow, he is able to know himself as a *self:* whole, unique, and mortal.

Section IV: "He is the end of things, the final man"

The peacefully detached self-knowledge reached in section III prepares for the remarkable transformation in section IV, where "I" disappears from the poem, dissolving into the contours of "the final man": the form in which each of us is embraced by the name *human.* "The lost self"—the mapless, snowbound self of the poem's opening—has changed in the process of turning open-eyed toward his death, the point where the river of consciousness meets the sea of oblivion. Renewed by acceptance of things as they are, he achieves another shape: that of the wisdom-figure, "An old man with his feet before the fire, / In robes of green, in garments of adieu." Roethke is careful to keep his characterization of "the final man" in this section simple and clear. He speaks in simple declarative sentences about his piercing love that wakes all the world's "loose wandering fire," and about his peace with himself:

> The murmur of the absolute, the why
> Of being born fails on his naked ears.
> His spirit moves like monumental wind
> That gentles on a sunny blue plateau.
> He is the end of things, the final man.

However, latent in these lines is another meaning, reserved for those with ears to hear. With the words "a sea-shape turning around," Roethke modulates from free verse into the rhythm of most metered English poetry from Chaucer's day to the present—blank verse (unrhymed iambic pentameter):

> A sea-shape turning around,—
> An old man with his feet before the fire,
> In robes of green, in garments of adieu.

Moreover, in these lines Roethke is unmistakably imitating the blank verse of a poet he revered and somewhat envied, Wallace Stevens. A reader would have to be very familiar with Wallace Stevens's poetry to know this. But clues abound: the use of a French word, common in Stevens but extremely rare in Roethke; the prominent use of two colors (Stevens consistently symbolized the imagination as blue, reality as green); references to "the final man" and "an old man with his feet before the fire"—images used by Stevens in such death-haunted poems as "Domination of Black," "Montrachet-le-Jardin," "Credences of Summer," "The Auroras of Autumn," and "Large Red Man Reading." Above all, it is the Stevensian use of the blank verse stanza that indicates his ghostly presence in "The Far Field." Compare Roethke's lines with these from Stevens's "Credences of Summer" and the impersonation becomes obvious:

> It is the natural tower of all the world,
> The point of survey, green's green apogee,
> But a tower more precious than the view beyond,
> A point of survey squatting like a throne,
> Axis of everything, green's apogee
>
> And happiest folk-land, mostly marriage-hymns.
> It is the mountain on which the tower stands,
> It is the final mountain. Here the sun,
> Sleepless, inhales his proper air, and rests.
> This is the refuge that the end creates.
>
> It is the old man standing on the tower,
> Who reads no book. His ruddy ancientness
> Absorbs the ruddy summer and is appeased,

By an understanding that fulfils his age,
By a feeling capable of nothing more.

Though blank verse exists as a resource in the English language itself, available to any poet, some poets use it so masterfully that it is reshaped and bears their signature. Shakespeare, Milton, and Wordsworth, to name the most influential, have all left their distinctive imprints on blank verse: we can speak of Shakespearian, Miltonic, or Wordsworthian blank verse and mean something that is quantifiable in the poetic lines. We can also say Stevensian blank verse, and mean something specific: blank verse presented in stanzas of lines with little enjambment, or running-on of sense past the end of the line; frequent use of anapests; frequent use of aphorisms ("this is the refuge that the end creates"); a diction that moves with casual ease from a specialized vocabulary ("green's green apogee . . . / Axis of everything") to common idiom ("happiest folk-land, mostly marriage-hymns")—all are characteristic of his style. Stevens, with his American voice, has altered blank verse; in "The Far Field" Roethke honors Stevens for this by imitating him—but only for a few lines. Having danced briefly to Stevens's rhythms in Stevens's symbols and style, Roethke moves to end the poem, with an audible feeling of power, in a voice that is distinctively his own, marked by frequent substitutions of trochees for iambs, with lines in parallel syntax enumerating and cataloging the minute particulars of the natural world. This is pure Roethke:

> All finite things reveal infinitude:
> The mountain with its singular bright shade
> Like the blue shine on freshly frozen snow,
> The after-light upon ice-burdened pines;
> Odor of basswood on a mountain-slope,
> A scent beloved of bees;
> Silence of water above a sunken tree:
> The pure serene of memory in one man,—
> A ripple widening from a single stone
> Winding around the waters of the world.

The ending of "The Far Field" is not merely a personal statement of belief in the power of the mind, facing death, to discover its place in the world. It is also a statement of belief in the power of art to communicate that discovery—to make maps and hand them on for refinement. Just as Stevens's poetry was for Roethke that precious kind of legacy, so

Roethke's poetry is meant to be for other generations of readers. Reading his poem, we not only bring his thought to life, we also validate his confidence. Moving outward from its source with the force of its beauty, insight, and love, the poem itself becomes the "ripple widening from a single stone / Winding around the waters of the world."

"Leah's eyes: ~~color~~ aura of riverwater;
of island willows trailing early green."

CHAPTER SIX

Making the Poem

To open a new book of poems, finding wide margins, handsome print, few words on each page—in comparison to a page of prose, with its imposing density of words—always fills me with a pleasurable sense of anticipation. I run my eye over the table of contents to get a sense, from the titles, of the poet's temperament and interests, and flip through the pages looking for short poems, to sample the poet's style. Then, if I'm attracted, I want to read the book from beginning to end.

I always read such a book, however, half-conscious of what it *won't* tell me. "Poetry" comes from the Greek word for making (*poiein:* to make). What we see on a printed page ought to be something thoroughly made: finished, and able to speak for itself. But we know that a poem often submits to many revisions before the poet lets it go from the workshop. What did the poet change, and why? What got the poem started? Why did it take this form? These are questions that only the poet can answer, if anyone. Yet in some sense the answers belong to the poem too, being part of its creation; and knowing the answers can give us insight into the creative process itself.

It seems fitting, then, to end this book with a brief discussion of the act of making poetry, to go behind the scenes and watch the processes that result in the finished product. The poems treated in this chapter are, necessarily, mine. I have chosen five that presented interesting problems—typical problems—solved in ways that satisfied me.

Writing a Poem in Meter with Rhymes

February Afternoon, In a Boat on the Seine
Leah's eyes: aura of riverwater;
Of island willows trailing early green;
Of the moss-garnished stone where water shatters,
Sunspray rushing in the rapid stream.

When my daughter, Leah, was four years old, we spent the winter traveling together in Europe. She always needed distraction at dinnertime in restaurants: drawing pictures, or making up stories and rhymes. One afternoon in Paris while we were taking a boat ride, I noticed that the gray-green of her eyes matched colors in the water and the young leaves budding on the willows of the Île de la Cité. I wrote out a few lines for that evening's entertainment:

> Leah's eyes—the color of riverwater,
> Of willow withes dividing winter light;
> Of the moss-garnished stone where water shatters;
> Of the moted bright.

Later, only one line and the rhyme pairing "water" with "shatters" seemed worth saving in their first form. Because I had chosen to write in meter, I had to negotiate the claims of both sound and sense. I wanted to make a poem that would integrate my impressions of the many resemblances between my daughter's eyes and the river in that weather. At the same time, I wanted to compose a flowing, falling, rushing rhythm evoking the sound of water. The last line represented a desperate settlement of the need for rhyme: a hackneyed "bright" to close up with "light." And many of the other words seemed either too self-conscious and arty—"willow withes dividing"; "moted"—or too flat: "color of riverwater."

In the final version, two changes please me very much. "Color" became "aura"—a word not only precise but also suggestive of many things I discovered I wanted to say once I had found that word. "Aura" means "a distinctive highly individualized atmosphere surrounding or attributed to a given source." It also means "a luminous radiation." In the context of the poem, the use of "aura" conveys something about the power of eyes. It was the sight of my daughter's eyes, so essential a link between herself and the world, that set the poem going in my mind. Not only the color of her eyes but their quickness and brightness were what I wanted to capture; I was seeing the world through them, and under their influence: Leah's aura.

"Rapid" also pleases me as a good addition to the poem, a word in which sound collaborates with sense to convey energy. Its sound pattern (trochaic) echoes that of many other two-syllable words in the poem: "Léah," "aúra," "ísland," "wíllows," "tráiling," "eárly," "gárnished," "wáter," "shátters," "súnspray," "rúshing." Adjectives are always spots in a line that need watching, like soft spots in fruit: the poem can go bad there. My early choice of "moted" is a good example: too decorative. "Rapid" not only filled out the rhythm as needed on the way to the closing rhyme; it also added information essential to the precision of the image.

Writing a Poem in Syllabics

Losing You

Winter; the woods
empty; the axe
sunk in a stump;
its thud a sob
startling the sleep
of the dreamer
waking, calling
Where am I? Who
is there?

This poem originated in a dream out of which I woke full of anxiety, sleeping one summer in a house in Massachusetts that stood near a large forest. The woods came into the dream, probably, under the influence of my grief at losing a person close to me: denuded trees and the sound of an axe falling seemed exactly the symbols I needed to express the emptiness I felt.

"Losing You" represents, I think, one of my most successful revisions. In its earliest version the line-endings were rather arbitrary; sometimes they coincided with units of syntax, sometimes not:

Winter; the woods
Empty; the axe
Buried in a stump;
Its fall become a sob in the sleep
Of the dreamer waking, calling out
Where am I? Who is there?

The demands of the syllabic form, once I decided on it, helped me purge the poem of dead language: "become," "in," "the," "out."

"Buried" became "sunk," discarding a syllable and gaining force in the process; "become" was exchanged for "startling." The rhythm produced by shortening the lines enhanced the feeling in the poem of being suddenly wakened into a terrible sort of questioning clarity. Getting rid of the capital letters conventionally placed at the head of lines also seemed to remove obstructions from what the poem was trying to say.

Writing a Poem with an Epigraph

Later

> *They brought me their comforts, and later*
> *They brought me their song.*
> Leonard Cohen, from "The Sisters of Mercy"

As you sing in the dark a room away tonight
Your voice drifts to me, ghostly, through the park.
We are in love. It is the third midnight.
Venus is high; the Bay gleams in the distance;
Our hands link lightly, and the fragrant grass
Offers a bed we know is ours, and soon.
The music retrieves it all. Your summoning voice
Is a path in the dark that leads me to this hill;
—The words hang in the air, the scene dissolves,
You sing, in the dark, a room away, tonight.

An epigraph makes a fine point of departure into a poem. Already formulated in attractive language, an epigraph can get things moving before the poem is really under way. An epigraph can set a mood; or it can be like the partner in a dialogue, starting an argument or posing a problem. Sometimes, like a good title, an epigraph can give intellectual orientation to the poem, conceptualizing a meaning the poet can't afford to put didactically. A good epigraph can be lifted from many sources: Mona Van Duyn in *Merciful Disguises* published a number of fine poems with epigraphs lifted from seed catalogs.

"Later" is a poem that originated in hearing a former lover sing a popular song that vividly brought back to me, listening, a scene from the past—though the singer, sitting a room away, was probably thinking of something else. The poem has meter, though no rhymes: five iambic beats per line, with frequent substitutions of anapests ("As you síng / in the dárk / a roóm / awáy / toníght"). I remember writing the first line first, just as it stands; the anapestic rhythm of Leonard Cohen's song probably guided my ear. While revising the poem I eventually made the rest of the lines take their rhythmic cues from that first line, although in several drafts the lines wobbled between free verse (without meter) and blank verse (iambic pentameter). This indecisiveness can still be felt in the second line, where "voice," "drifts," and "to" all want to receive stresses; however, this tension pleases me as a rhythmic effect.

Writing a Free Verse Poem in Units of Syntax

Gin Considered as a Demon

Incubus, she invites you.
Kindle her body with cold.
Rise in her like a muscular dancer. Narrow the light
So a single beam shines on the floor of her brain.
In the chill circle of blue, possessed,
For hours she will leap and pirouette
With you, the ghostly lover
Lost in her blood.
Later, as her eyes close,
Whisper with icy breath about the distance between stars
And how deep the frost reaches into the ground tonight.

"Gin Considered as a Demon" is about a woman who has taken alcohol for a lover. The poem describes her addiction as a strenuous dance with an invisible partner—an incubus, or erotic demon—whose seductions lead toward death.

The poem is visually so concrete that I wanted nothing to interfere with the presentation of the movement of bodies through space. I let the lines fall as naturally as possible into speech units, lengthening and shortening them in a way I hoped would underscore the choreography of the imagery: the formal movement of dancers reaching out, lifting themselves, and stepping back. In an early version of the poem I gave the imperative verbs parallel places at the head of three lines: "kindle," "rise," and "narrow" were lined up like commands, with "Narrow the light" standing as a line all its own. I think the later version, where a sentence ends in the middle of the line, is rhythmically more interesting because less mechanical.

The poem has neither meter nor rhyme to provide an overall pattern of recurring sound. Instead, a sound structure emerges as the ear detects the emphatic presence of assonance—recurring vowel sounds in stressed syllables—drawing the lines together auditorily, as rhyme would do. Key words in the poem are "chill" and "icy." The short *i* and long *i* in those words is repeated over and over, often in combination with *n*, making an off-rhyme: "gin," "considered," "incubus," "invites," "kindle," "single"; "whisper," "distance"; "chill," "will," "pirouette." The long *i*, though less frequent, echoes from the first line to the last, in "invite," "like," "light," "shines," "eyes," "icy," "tonight."

"Gin Considered as a Demon" profited very much from the amputation of a line. Originally the poem ended—and I hate to admit it—

> Tell her with icy breath about the distance between stars
> And how deep the frost reaches into the ground tonight;
> Into her unfilled grave.

Too melodramatic. I think I made the poem more, rather than less, terrifying by dropping this line. Cosmic emptiness supplies a more resonant image for the experience of demonic possession one can get from sipping from a chill circle of gin, with its faintly blue cast, than any mere reference to a grave.

Writing an Egoless Poem

Carl Uncovers a Bed of Wild Strawberries

> The sun beats straight down. Carl
> Scythes the standing grass
> Unstoppering stems like bottles:
> Borage, timothy, foxtails, even the nettles
> Send their perfumes, green, green,
> Straight up shafts of sunlight streaming through trees
> Where Carl, stooping,
> Uncovers this hidden fruit and gathers it:
> Another unsought gift.

This is a poem from a group titled "Family Portraits," in which I tried to capture glimpses of other people's lives, keeping myself out of the picture. Here I describe someone performing what used to be a quite common chore; I find in the poem a faint nostalgia I didn't know I was feeling. However, the effect I hoped to achieve was what Wallace Stevens in *The Necessary Angel* calls "transparency": the lines become a frame, the poet's words the medium through which *things* are seen without intrusion by a commentator. The poet's presence is felt in the intensity of the perceptions. In "Carl Uncovers a Bed of Wild Strawberries," intensity is conveyed in the use of repetition ("green, green") and certain types of particularity ("straight up"; "straight down"; emphatic use of names). But there is no "I" in the poem.

Some of the revisions discussed in this chapter occurred to me in the course of preparing these poems for inclusion here. In *revision* the poet literally takes another look at what the poem says, with an eye to making it more true to its own terms. No matter how powerful the inspiration that gets the poem started, the power of the poem will be that of its language. And the play with words can itself bring the writer great satisfaction. For writing poetry is a way of making vivid inner worlds reveal their content. A notebook of poems can become for the writer an archive of mental states explored and outlived—a record of the processes by which we move from one point of view to another in our efforts to make personal sense of our worlds.

I invite you, in closing, to put pencil to paper and undertake some revelations of your own.

Reader's Guide

READERS INTERESTED in the poets, poems, and issues discussed in this book may want to pursue their interests further. This section provides titles of books, articles, and essays addressed to the general reader, listed under the relevant chapter headings; it also provides attribution of fuller sources for quotations in the chapter where needed, and acknowledgements of books that shaped my thinking about the chapters' themes.

Chapter One

For further reading in modern poetry two anthologies are especially useful because they include a very large number of poets, and supply helpful introductory notes:

The Norton Anthology of Modern Poetry, edited by Richard Ellmann and Robert O'Clair (New York: W.W. Norton, 1973).

The Voice That Is Great Within Us, edited by Hayden Carruth (New York: Bantam, 1970).

For interesting reading on poetics (the theory of poetry), with special emphasis on modern poetry, see:

Harvey Gross, *Sound and Form in Modern Poetry* (Ann Arbor: The University of Michigan Press, 1968).

James McMichael, *The Style of the Short Poem* (Belmont, Ca.: Wadsworth, 1967).

The Imagist Poem: Modern Poetry in Miniature, edited by William Pratt (New York: E.P. Dutton, 1963).

The Poetics of the New American Poetry, edited by Donald M. Allen and Warren Tallman (New York: Grove Press, 1973).

Princeton Encyclopedia of Poetry and Poetics, edited by Alex Preminger (Princeton: Princeton University Press, 1974).

Charles Rosen's comments on techniques of composition leading to free verse were excerpted from his article "The Origins of Walter Benjamin," *The New York Review of Books,* vol. 25, no. 18, November 10, 1977.

Discussion of the process of unfolding the poem at four different levels—autonomous, contextual, biographical, and affective—is modeled on Richard L. McGuire's chapter "Ways of Seeing" in *Passionate Attention: An Introduction to Literary Study* (New York: W.W. Norton, 1973), and on M.H. Abrams's "Introduction: Orientation of Critical Theories" in *The Mirror and the Lamp: Romantic Theory and the Critical Tradition* (New York: W.W. Norton, 1958).

Chapter Two

Dylan Thomas has been the subject of many books; I recommend: Donald Hall, *Remembering Poets* (New York: Harper & Row, 1978); Paul Ferris, *Dylan Thomas* (New York: Dial, 1977); and *Selected Letters of Dylan Thomas,* edited by Constantine FitzGibbon (New York: New Directions, 1967).

My understanding of William Wordsworth's "Ode: Intimations of Immortality" is indebted to Lionel Trilling's essay "The Immortality Ode" in *The Liberal Imagination* (New York: Viking, 1942).

Influencing my discussion of the interrelation of childhood and adult life in this chapter and in Chapter Five were two books by Erik Erikson: *Childhood and Society* (New York: W.W. Norton, 1963) and *Toys and Reasons: Stages in the Ritualization of Experience* (New York: W.W. Norton, 1976).

Chapter Three

Excellent general discussions of the life and work of William Butler Yeats are Richard Ellmann, *Yeats: The Man and the Masks* (New York: Macmillan, 1948), and Louise MacNeice, *The Poetry of W.B. Yeats* (New York: Oxford University Press, 1967). A useful collection of critical essays, containing a good bibliography, is *William Butler Yeats,* edited by Patrick J. Keane (New York: McGraw-Hill, 1973).

Louise Bogan's letters are printed in *What the Woman Lived: Selected Letters of Louise Bogan 1920–1970,* edited by Ruth Limmer (New York: Harcourt Brace Jovanovich, 1973).

"The Idea of Hawk," by James McConkey, is quoted from *The New Yorker,* vol. 54, June 26, 1978.

Important to my thinking about the theme of self-liberation in this chapter was Ernest Becker, *The Denial of Death* (New York: Free Press, 1973).

Chapter Four

The majority of critical books on Sylvia Plath tend to be interpretations of her suicide rather than her poetry. A noteworthy exception is Judith Kroll, *Chapters in a Mythology: The Poetry of Sylvia Plath* (New York: Harper & Row, 1976). The commentary of Sylvia Plath on her own poetry, quoted in this chapter, was excerpted from tapes of interviews accompanying readings by Plath made by the British Council shortly before her death, and quoted by A. Alvarez in his essay "Sylvia Plath," in *The Art of Sylvia Plath,* edited by Charles Newman (Bloomington: Indiana University Press, 1970).

Anne Sexton's remarks on confessional poetry are from a transcription of a videotaped interview conducted by William Heyen and A. Poulin, Jr., in *American Poets in 1976* (Indianapolis: Bobbs-Merrill, 1976). Quotations from Anne Sexton's letters are from *Anne Sexton: A Self-Portrait in Letters,* edited by Linda Gray Sexton and Lois Ames (Boston: Houghton Mifflin, 1977).

Adrienne Rich's development as a poet is the subject of a fine critical essay by David Kalstone in *Five Temperaments* (New York: Oxford University Press, 1977). Rich's essay "When We Dead Awaken" is reprinted in *Adrienne Rich's Poetry,* selected and edited by Barbara Charlesworth Gelpi and Albert Gelpi (New York: W.W. Norton, 1975).

Chapter Five

A good general discussion of Roethke's poetry is Karl Malkoff, *Theodore Roethke* (New York: Columbia University Press, 1966).

My discussion of the structure of the meditative poem is indebted to Louis Martz, *The Poetry of Meditation* (New Haven: Yale University Press, 1954).

Chapter Six

Interesting commentaries by poets on the making of their own poems may be found in *Fifty Contemporary Poets: The Creative Process* (New York: David McKay, 1977), and *Poet's Choice,* edited by Paul Engle and Joseph Langland (New York: Dell, 1962).

INDEX

INDEX